The Orphans of Tar – A Speculative Opera

Julien de Smet, Ronny Heiremans, Heike Langsdorf, Vanessa Müller, Filip Van Dingenen, Stijn Van Dorpe, Clémentine Vaultier, Katleen Vermeir

2

An Introduction to the Book Series and to the Third Book

Choreography as Conditioning is a series of five books conceived and realized in the framework of the artistic research project "Distraction as Discipline".[1] Throughout the forty months in which this project has been realized, and as one of its constitutive components, different groups of artist researchers have been invited to write *through* their practices, that is, to depart from collective artistic practices and to let these practices generate reflections, ideas, concepts, and (written) material. 'Choreography' is understood here in its widest sense, as a way of organizing subjects in their surroundings, while 'conditioning' refers to inducing states or situations we experience every day. Where, how, and by whom do things get organized, and what kinds of landscapes of experience are made im/possible by the practices we encounter in our (working) lives?

What 'choreography' points to, as well, is both the collective character of these processes ("choreo-") and the generation of diverse kinds of signs ("-graphy"). 'Conditioning' implies the same two semantic elements: collectivity ("con-") and the production of, in this case linguistic, oral signs ("ditioning-" from "dicere": to say). Accordingly, each book in this series addresses different thematic fields on the basis of the collective, intertwined, connected performance of different artistic research practices in different constellations and the resulting generation of artifacts—in this case, texts. The ground on which this book series emerges is therefore an open-ended, dynamic network of relational practices. The books themselves become part of this network with the aim of keeping the processes alive, and thus open. To do so, the process should remain 'vague enough' in order to assume an observational attitude and to enable variable insights, trajectories, and inquiries, of people moving and being moved, sensing, thinking, and acting. This requires space and time for requestioning by remembering, and avoids that a given landscape of ideas is confirmed or consolidated too hastily.

This third book, which appears right in the middle of the series, coheres with this approach exemplarily: it is inconclusive. It presents, at once, the success and the danger of thoughts creating volumes, personalities, and possible courses of action. *The Orphans of Tar – A Speculative Opera* answers the question posed in the second book *(Practicing Futures through Voicing)* by transforming life into voices and presenting possible mindsets through co-authoring a factual iction. As such, it constitutes a mental space in which fictitious characters find an almost disturbing expansion of their thoughts. Accordingly, the book can be considered as an allegory of human thoughts as (possible) actions: what *could* happen becomes what *does* happen.

Thoughts embodied through conversation co-create realities. Whether it is wanted or not, they—both thoughts and realities—literally 'infect' each other. Through their interaction, they enable unforeseen and unforeseeable conceptions, imaginations, and prospects. For better and worse.

We want to thank Katleen Vermeir and Ronny Heiremans for their always rigorous artistic way of proceeding; Antony Hudek, Lars Kwakkenbos, Peter Westenberg, Emmanuel Depoorter and Danielle van Zuijlen for supporting, hosting, and joining the workshop at KASK and Kunsthal Gent in which this book is rooted; and Julien de Smet, Vanessa Müller, Filip Van

Dingenen, Stijn Van Dorpe and Clémentine Vaultier
for together processing a large number of concepts
and possible directions that ended up becoming
the speculative opera you can now "read".

Alex Arteaga & Heike Langsdorf

---

1. 'Distraction as Discipline – An investigation into the function of attention and participation in performance art and art pedagogy / Langsdorf & Luyten 2016 – 2019

6

On Co-authoring a Factual Fiction

This publication results from a workshop by Vermeir & Heiremans for students of Autonomous Design and Curatorial Studies at KASK Ghent, by invitation of Heike Langsdorf in the context of her series of working moments and writing processes *Choreography as Conditioning*.

The workshop focussed on the growing financialization of the arts, urban space, and daily life—themes on which the artist duo has been working since 2006. During the work sessions, the participants reflected on art's role in the production (and possible distribution) of value in today's artistic and non-artistic realms and on possibilities to enhance the sustainability of artistic practices.

As a case-study for the workshop, Vermeir & Heiremans invited PILOOT,[1] a group of artists that is developing long-term artistic reflections and exercises in response to this situation, which started as a public art commission in 2015 by the city of Ghent and the real estate development Tondelier.[2] Danielle van Zuijlen, Filip Van Dingenen and Stijn Van Dorpe were invited to the workshop to present this long-term project and share their involvement in it.

For this art commission, PILOOT curator Danielle van Zuijlen proposed not to realize a single art work, but instead to create an 'artistic platform' in relation to the Tondelier site that could engage with the Rabot neighbourhood over a long-term period. Rabot is considered a vulnerable area. Hoping to bridge—and reflect on—the gap between the still to be created more affluent development within the Rabot area, she invited five artists who realized site-specific interventions that often involve the local community. To be able to continue their long-term 'exercises' related to the site, the artists and the curator proposed to integrate their new artistic platform in the (semi-) public space of the Tondelier site as a new 'utility'— parallel to services like rubbish collection or childcare— or perhaps as a 'third space', a term that was often used during the workshop by Vermeir & Heiremans.[3] During the process, the idea was proposed to establish a special art fund that would grow by receiving a percentage of the sales of the new apartments. This fund was intended to sustain the platform in the long run. Surplus value generated by artistic practices and community efforts could flow back to the creators of that value, which would be a basis for a more sustainable artistic platform on the site, and have valuable effects for the whole neighborhood.

After the workshop at KASK, the group felt the need to continue the conversation and their search for possible 'third spaces'. Heike Langsdorf's invitation to make a publication rooted in the workshop was extended to everyone participating in the post-workshop meetings, and a co-authored process of discussion and writing ensued. In the following pages, you can read a selection of the transcriptions of these meetings.

1. "Art in Public Space," https://www.flandersartsinstitute.be/research-and-development/art-in-public-space/5176-art-in-the-public-space-eight-recommendations-regarding-policy-and-practice ((accessed 08.09.2019) and "Meer dan object," Issuu, pp. 91-94, https://issuu.com/vlaamsbouwmeester/docs/kio_web (accessed 08.09.2019).
2. "Over Tondelier," https://www.tondelier.be/nl/over-tondelier (accessed 29.08.2019).
3. "Cultural Diversity and Cultural Differences," Atlas of Transformation, http://monumenttotransformation.org/atlas-of-transformation/html/c/cultural-diversity/cultural-diversity-and-cultural-differences-homi-k-bhabha.html (accessed 29.08.2019).

31.03.2019
REPORT ON THE 1ST THIRD SPACE MEETING / KUNSTHAL GENT

We discuss a speculative future in which the *PILOOT* platform at Tondelier has become a reality. We also want to go beyond this fiction, and to think about ways to develop possible 'third spaces'.

> **Vanessa:**
> "A 'third space' is a safe space, a playground, where a discussion can be held without putting the ever-delusional reality (e.g. existing institutions) first. It is a space of futurology and fiction that allows participants to play with scenarios in an airy (virtual) environment off the grid. This is why fictive storytelling is a perfect medium to create a 'third space'. As Friedrich Torberg says in *Ballade der großen Müdigkeit*, '…Ich möchte gern zwei kleine Hunde sein und miteinander spielen.'"[1]

Our discussions about a 'third space' consider establishing a mental space, rather than a physical space, for exchanging ideas. We come to the idea of writing an 'opera' together. Based on what we experienced during the workshop (facts and contexts), we initiate a dialogue that can introduce fictional elements.

> **Vanessa:**
> Since a lot of insights and stories that Filip and the other artists shared, sound like the perfect template for writing an opera/operetta/musical/trailer for an upcoming Broadway play, *Tondelier,* from the makers of *Les Miserables,* I would propose to attempt to either write a 'scene' or a 'review/critique' about the opening night of that play. I can already see the play's characters: Pigeons, Caterpillars, Micro-Currency, and The Palace of Justice."

15.05.2019
REPORT ON THE 2ND THIRD SPACE MEETING / SCHAARBEEK

We are looking for a way, a structure, or a method for 'writing' together.

> **Filip:**
> "Umberto Eco argues in his text *The Poetics of the Open Work* that Brecht's play does not devise solutions at all. It ends in a situation of ambiguity and it is thus up to the audience to draw their own conclusions. Here the work is 'open' in the same sense that a debate is 'open'. A solution is seen as desirable and is actually anticipated, but it must come from the audience. In this case, the 'openness' is converted into an instrument of revolutionary pedagogics."[2]

We come to the conclusion that we should write our factual fiction from many different perspectives, all of which would reference a central point. The film *Rashomon* is mentioned as an example. In Kurosawa's film, different perspectives on the central plot of the film are narrated without offering a comprehensive conclusion or truth.[3] We discuss how our different stories could be linked to each other. Do we need one common detail to start from?

We consider other principles for writing.
    One could be *cadavre exquis:* we all write a part and we distribute the writing to one another and add to it without reading what was written before, so that a surprising pattern of text can develop.[4]
    Another option could be to start from a 'common paragraph'. All stories would 'pass through' this paragraph at a certain point in the different narrations.

We decide to do each other's editing, so writing becomes a real *co*-writing process. Other games, similar to *cadavre exquis,* are mentioned but we decide against using them. We all start from the different perspectives we have on the Tondelier topic. These texts will go back and forth in a co-writing and co-editing process.

> **Clémentine:**
> "Kenneth Goldsmith questions authorship and is a so-called 'uncreative writer'.[5] He says that we all appropriate from each other, and that all our ideas are second-hand. He proposes to think of the context as the new content. He uses existing texts and considers the author as a dj who 'samples' depending on the context. The sampling is the creative part. The 'uncreative' part relates to the fact that we should acknowledge we always borrow from others."[6]

We consider how fiction is part and parcel of the real estate industry's projections for developments, well before the building process has started. We contrast these projections with the realities we observed on site, such as the huge machines cleaning the land and the awful stench of tar that suffocates the neighborhood.

We remind ourselves of many details of the site that were once a reality before the real estate projections. Tondelier had communal gardens for the people living in the Rabot neighborhood. To create incentives for people to work on the land, the city of Ghent introduced a complementary currency–*Torekes*.[7] Only these could be used to rent the gardens. This top down model of social engineering had an impact and improved life at Rabot.

We imagine the plants that are now trying to come back through the tar. A text by Donna Haraway is mentioned.

> **Filip:**
> *"The Children of Compost* is an inter-species fable for making a liveable world for all. The stories trace five *Camilles* from 2025 to 2425, a period in which the human population, having at first risen from eight to ten billion, dropped to three billion, with only half of the species that existed in 2015 still alive. Many humans have been modified to take on aspects of other species; in the case of the *Camilles,* it is the monarch butterfly."[8]

We want to integrate ideas that we have been developing around the notion of a 'third space'. We think that this could keep our common practice alive, both physically as well as philosophically: a possibility for common actions, an institution created bottom up, changing relationships and value systems, eliminating criteria for inclusion or exclusion.

> **Stijn:**
> "Because this idea of a 'third space' keeps surfacing, I would like to share a text that I wrote half a year ago. It somehow draws out what makes the term relevant for me, or rather where 'third spaces' (I really prefer to use the plural form) emerge for me."[9]

In our stories, we want to integrate 'third spaces'—those that do not exist (yet).

One example: it was the CEO of Tondelier Development, who came up with the idea to create a fund that would enable the continuation of the artistic platform on the site. It was his idea that these activities could be funded partly by the sales of the apartments on the development site.

The CEO even came up with a possible other project, but one that he feared tremendously. He was very worried that someone would propose to open up the former Canal De Lieve that runs invisibly underground, through the future inner garden of the Tondelier real estate development. In their projected artist impressions, the company instead included an artificial water pond.

Lotte Geeven, one of the artists of *PILOOT,* had proposed *The Golden Apartment.*[10] This project would create the possibility for everyone—including less affluent citizens—to acquire having a stake in the real estate, by buying a tiny part, a share, of the apartment. Could those citizens from then on influence what could happen on the location?

A rumor was circulating that the local Rabot church was purchased by the developers to create a new community centre. It turned out that it was the city of Ghent that had bought the church.

> **Stijn:**
> "Because I could hardly believe it, I checked the news. It's the city of Ghent who bought the church and it's the city who will turn it into a social centre ('ontmoetingscentrum'). That was also the reason that Oryx kept the 'gas meters' out of the project—to externalize the investment and socialize the costs by sending the bill to the City. It made sociologist Pascal Gielen furious during a meeting at the atelier of the 'master builder' ('bouwmeester')."[11]

All these examples create possibilities for a more equitable distribution of resources. The artists working on site and the people living at Rabot have created a lot of extra value and positive attention for the site through art projects and gardening, but this surplus value is absorbed by the new real estate owners. The creation of a fund based on a percentage of the sales contracts could distribute these values more evenly, and would include the originators of those values.

We recognize that there is a 'third space' in what we have created together so far—a long-term collaboration in which we are thinking about an ecology of practices. How can we further integrate and develop our ideas on these 'third spaces'?

01 – 03.07.2019
REPORT ON THE 3ʳᴰ THIRD SPACE MEETINGS / GHENT, ELSENE, SCHAARBEEK

Based on our discussion during a previous gathering, we decide to write an opera.

We agree that we need to define a number of characters.

We agree to write one common paragraph that will return in all contributions. The form this will take remains open.

We agree that there will be individual contributions that together form a multi-perspective narrative.

We ask ourselves if the opera could one day be performed (for example in a garden, on a metaphorical location, or a situated location)?

> **Ronny:**
> "There would be an early morning soundscape of birds, a tsunamic sound wave of bird twitter; there would be the echoes of stones.[12] There would be white noise concerts with people from the surrounding streets who enter the story as co-writers…"

We discuss different aspects of our opera's setting: the olfactory (the smell of the Tondelier construction site);

the visual (it could be a 'fruit forest'); the temporal (forget about linear time—our story comes to us from different moments).

We randomly remember 'things' we have talked about before.

"Where is the Tondelier reality? We don't want it to become a mere fiction, but rather a fictionalization of ourselves. We could interview each other and deploy 'interaction' as the main characteristic of the framework of our writing."

"Where is our Monopoly game? The game we played to present the workshop outcome, if that was what it was?"

"Where's what we named the 'third space'? Is it the tension between the writing process (imagined reality) and real elements (mundane reality)? Imagination while writing somehow has to do with our specific reality. It is writing through practice. Maybe the 'third space' is the shared paragraph that we mentioned earlier on?"

"Is it not happening right now? How can we connect it to the actual writing? How can we inhabit the 'third space', the location, the metaphor, the garden?"

"There is a lot of pressure on the 'third space' as a space for doubt, also a space in the context of arts education. The space for doubting has sometimes become a 'career space'. It is an active space that needs to be defended, but other incentives have come into the pedagogical environment. How can we resist this?"

"How to develop our opera characters? What makes the character singular, and what ends up in the common paragraph?"

"The opera could play anywhere. It does not need a fixed place. We could do it in this drama studio, or in a garden."

"The recurring paragraph constructs the framework of the opera, with all evolving around these words. The rhythm of the Monopoly game could be part of that framework: opportunity, transaction, consequence."

We are constructing characters. Everyone thinks of
properties for a certain character. We introduce the
profiles to the group. We decide to add characteristics
through a game on the principle of 'Russian Roulette'.
We don't use a gun, but a kitchenknife. We place it on
the table and spin it. Each round is about one of the
profiles. The person to whom the knife points can add
or subtract from the character of the one who spun it.

    We name the characters of the opera:

> Miss Trust
> Lobbyist From The Grave
> The People
> Shareholder Activists
> The Set
> Anxious Explorer
> UAP
> Tar

We decide not to write one common paragraph of the
opera together. Instead, we aim for a 'common ground'
around which all the characters could come together.
    This common ground can be integrated within
each character's development.
    The common space is an empty plot in which
all (conflicting) interests become manifest. The empty
plot is a narrative space representing the Tondelier site:
it can contain the mountains of sand, tar, and the artist
project *The Golden Apartment*. But mostly it is a place
of becoming.

> **Ronny:**
> "Maybe it's a good idea not to write an elaborate
> story with characters, but instead to refer to the
> theatre piece by Luigi Pirandello, *Six Characters
> in Search of an Author,* [13] which includes

the meta story of a theater play, combined with
a suicide story."

Although conditions of production are often not visible, or
people are not interested in them, we find these conditions
important enough to include some of the notes that were
taken throughout the writing process.

Our opera will probably include an introduction,
character descriptions, and meta-stories that give insight
in how the process of writing evolved.

Clémentine:

"I like the real estate advertisements we talked
about, these so-called artist impressions inspire me
a lot. As an artist, do you want to work with the
dark side of 'gentrification' or with the 'commons'?
This is roughly paraphrasing what we mentioned
before. In any case, I am thinking about what kind
of artist impressions we can offer in that sense.

I love the lyrical idea of an opera with
butterflies and multi-wheeled rollers on a post-
apocalyptic worksite. This sounds obviously super
great to me!

I can see that all of this is 'mixing' very
well with my impression of the construction site as
an undiscovered island filled with wild birds and
insects, and obviously with an unstable geology!
A land to be conquered by brave travellers who
settle as a colony of 'golden apartments'! I am
curious about what kind of artist impressions drove
them here."

16.07.2019
REPORT ON THE 4TH THIRD SPACE MEETING / SCHAARBEEK

Next to our character descriptions, we consider to write a part in which each of us presents his or her own perspective on the other characters. This would also include excerpts of the narrative of the opera and descriptions of what the characters are doing.

    Only The Set will not have this relational aspect. The Set is described as a condition that makes the interactions of the others possible. "Nothing is owned by me, but I am involved in everything."[14]

> **Clémentine:**
> "While writing, I thought of the following references: *Utopia,* the book by Thomas Moore, in which through speculation an ideal society is spatially situated in a far away colony[15] and *Crash Park,* a play by Philippe Quesne about survivors of a plane crash on a virgin island.[16]

We discuss whether all the notes we take during all our sessions, or only a part of them, should be included in the opera script. We decide to include the relational part in the development of the characters and, although we find all perspectives interesting, we think that using all the notes would be too much. A selection of the notes is sufficient to make the writing process transparent. It details how we 'organized' our collective writing process and exposes the discussions and methods that eventually lead to the development of a number of characters.

> **Katleen's addition to the UAP:**
> "For me, the connection of the UAP with the Feng Shui specialist is important. He is

> an ambiguous figure. In Asia, he is at the same time considered a spiritual person who knows the power of the flow of the air. At the same time, a positive report of the Feng Shui specialist generates an enhancement of real estate values. If he comes up with a negative report, it can still be transformed into a good one when one pays more than initially bargained for."

We discuss if our narratives need an introduction / contextualization, yet not giving away the story. How to make it readable without explaining too much?

We entertain the idea of an epilogue by Danielle. It positions her at arm's length and positively supports her idea to write a contribution from the perspective she has on the process. For her, this makes sense as she did not take part in the writing process. As the curator of *PILOOT,* she can bridge earlier stages of the project with our ideas of 'third spaces'.

We talk about all footnotes that we will use in the text, all the references to books and essays. We consider the possibility to create a 'library', real or virtual, at Kunsthal.

'Third spaces' can be seen as temporalities and energies coming together: those emanating from the workshop, those at the Tondelier site, and those in our co-writing meetings. It is 'a choreography as conditioning': moving through the conditions of writing together. It is a situated practice. What we write is not just a fiction, it derives from our experiences at different moments in different places that we are now collectivizing through writing. We could speak of finding alternatives through creating 'third spaces'. In design, this is called prototyping. It is not something static, but a constant modeling and rescaling of the research questions…

Clémentine's addition to Miss Trust:
"Miss Trust could meet the Lobbyist From The Grave and fall in love with the dilemma embodied in his skills. He is charismatic, yet detached. They could meet in a park in an artist impression. They could meet in *The Golden Apartment*. Is it becoming a cage? What would she do with this place? Does she own it, or is she waiting for it to be sold? She can be the daughter of a powerful person."

Stijn's addition to Miss Trust:
"What about the social gap with The People? They have the open space of the construction site in between them; one could say that they have it in common, but they cannot claim ownership of it."

Katleen's addition to Miss Trust:
"I am thinking of a link between Miss Trust and an art trust. A body that could make the art production on Tondelier more sustainable. Miss Trust reminds me of Virginia Dwan, who owned Dwan Gallery. She was the heir of a mining business, 3M, and it is through her that Robert Smithson's work, and other land art projects, became possible."[17]

02.08.2019
REPORT ON THE 5TH THIRD SPACE MEETING / SCHAARBEEK

We are reading out loud together all the character contributions and we comment on the narratives. How do characters relate to other characters? How do they relate to the existing Tondelier site, to our plot, to The Set?

How do characters unfold and embody our discussions?

We confirm our decision to describe the writing process and start working on a first draft.

> **Filip's contribution to The Set:**
> "If The Set is mute, it should think about a relation to tone and vibration. I am thinking about a metabolism! The garden is not growing, but rather digesting, burp!"
>
> **Clémentine:**
> "I'm referring to Flaubert's last book *Bouvard and Pécuchet*.[18] It is about two Parisian copyists who decide to move to the countryside. Their search for intellectual stimulation leads them, over the course of several years, to flounder through almost every branch of knowledge. Each chapter is revolving around a field of knowledge. For example they start a farm, and become passionate about gardening, gradually expanding to other fields. They fail in all their efforts. It is very inspiring to see how Flaubert's work process of adding, accumulating, connecting knowledges, seeps into the structure of the book. For Flaubert, the book is a pretext for learning."
>
> I also want to reflect on the structure of the final book. The introduction contextualizes Flaubert's work process, the story itself, the scenario, and the copy (an accumulation of quotes that Flaubert came across, reproduced and lived with. It is where the research of Flaubert and that of the copyist fuse. On the one hand, there is the story 'about', and on the other hand there is the underlying research of a copyist who actually has to *read* in order to create his story).
>
> Disgusted with the world in general, Bouvard and Pécuchet ultimately decide

> "(…) to return to copying as before", giving
> up their intellectual blundering. Originally, it
> was intended that the last chapter would be
> followed by a large sample of what they copy:
> possibly a 'sottisier' (an anthology of stupid
> quotations), *Dictionary of Received Ideas*
> (an encyclopaedia of commonplace notions),
> or a combination of both."

For the publication, we talk about the possibilities for printing the two different types of texts (the characters and the notes). Texts on the characters could run on all even pages, and the notes on all uneven pages. This way, the reader always has an eye on both the process of writing the opera and on how we transform 'ourselves', our dialogues, into the different 'characters'.

12.08.2019
REPORT ON THE 6TH THIRD SPACE MEETING / SCHAARBEEK

One of Filip's proposals for *PILOOT* was to literally follow the tar polluted soil to where it would be stored or purified. He reads fragments of the email exchanges he had with the companies Aclagro,[19] Oryx,[20] Tondelier Development[21] and Injectis[22] dating from 2017. He is asking them if he could join the tar-filled boats to their final destination. One director refers him to the next, and eventually he is denied access to the tar transportations altogether.

Katleen shows diagrams of the networks the companies Tondelier Development[23] and Koramic Real Estate[24] are inscribed in. She found the diagrams on the website of the *Belgisch Staatsblad/Belgian Official Gazette*. For her, this diagram represents a characteristic of the Shareholder Activists, being a networked entity.

Stijn's addition to the Shareholder Activists:
"I would suggest that the character has also another quality than only being interested in investing. Perhaps it is also interested in meditation or yoga. I propose to take some inspiration from the book *Less is Enough: On Architecture and Asceticism* by Pier Vittorio Aureli."[25]

Heike's addition to the Shareholder Activists:
"What the Lobbyist From The Grave has in common with the Shareholder Activists is that they all are interested in who is in power and what that power does. They find out what those in power do, and where they are. They follow the money in order to find the people or the other way around."

Ronny's addition to The People:
"The People are the stakeholders, those that create value, but do not share in the value. The People have been or have depoliticized themselves, because they have listened to the sirens of populism. This has further deteriorated their position. The ultimate question with which The People see themselves confronted is how to take control and whether this involves a political process or violent action. Either way, this process can only start if certain conditions have been fulfilled: awareness and urgency.

We discuss the idea of a map visualizing the relations between the different characters. Inspired by the Shareholder Activists, we decide to produce one, possibly to be printed on an inside cover unfolding from the book.

To create this map, we choose 30 to 40 keywords from the different character descriptions, terms that each character senses to be of paramount importance to the other characters. The keywords will be run through an algorithm, to constitute the relations between the characters, their situations, and contexts.

Will this algorithmic machine device 'flatten' our narratives? Or do we consider it a tool for speculative writing? The setting of the parameters would seem essential.

Could this be part of The Set, encompassing all of the characters and all their permutations? We decide to print all eight maps on top of each other.

> **Julien's addition to the Lobbyist from the Grave:**
> "He has several cancers. A brain cancer caused the frontal cortex to be partially removed. It was pressing on the optical nerve, and that left him colour blind in his left eye."

We discuss a title for our opera.

We discuss the printed order of appearance of the characters in the publication.

Does Tar come at the end, or is Tar absent altogether? Do The People come after the Lobbyist From The Grave, as he mentions them in the very end? Is The Set after the Shareholder Activists, as this would create a very logical transition? Should the Anxious Explorer follow The Set, as we can imagine her literally flying into the 'image'?

> **Filip:**
> "The title of the opera could be *The Orphans of Tar*." [26]

> **Vanessa:**
> "The refrain of the Opera's choir could be this:
>
> Opportunity:
> Eruption, Corruption,
> there is always an option.
> Money they chase.

Purification is not the case.

Transaction:
Black is the ground.
Transformation takes time.
And is never just found.

Consequence:
Turn the stone.
The alchemist will know.
Adding or taking.
The future will show."

1. Friedrich Torberg, "Ballade der großen Müdigkeit," in *Auch Nichtraucher müssen sterben: Essays-Feuilletons-Notizen-Glossen* (München: Langen Müller, 1985). Translation: "I would like to be two little dogs and play together."
2. "Umberto Eco, The Open Work," Icosilune, http://www.icosilune.com/2008/08/umberto-eco-the-open-work/ (accessed 29.08.2019). Note: *Opera aperta* 1962, rev. 1976; English translation: *The Open Work* (1989). *The Open Work* is Umberto Eco's first book on the subject of semiotics. Eco is concerned with the evolution and values of open works, where openness is understood as freedom of interpretation and meaning making. Openness is dependent on the freedom of an observer to interpret or explore meaning within a work.
3. Wikipedia. 2019. "Rashomon." https://en.wikipedia.org/wiki/Rashomon (accessed 29.08.2019). Note: *Rashomon* is a 1950 Jidaigeki film (period drama) directed by Akira Kurosawa, working in close collaboration with cinematographer Kazuo Miyagawa. The film is known for a plot device that involves various characters providing subjective, alternative, self-serving, and contradictory versions of the same incident. Rashomon marked the entrance of Japanese film onto the world stage.
4. Wikipedia. 2019. "Exquisite Corpse." https://en.wikipedia.org/wiki/Exquisite_corpse (accessed 29.08.2019). Note: Exquisite corpse, also known as exquisite cadaver (from the original French term cadavre exquis), is a method by which a collection of words or images is collectively assembled. Each collaborator adds to a composition in sequence, either by following a rule or by being allowed to see only the end of what the previous person contributed. This technique was invented by the surrealists and the name is derived

from a phrase that resulted when they first played the game, "Le cadavre exquis boira le vin nouveau." ("The exquisite corpse shall drink the new wine.")

5. Kenneth Goldsmith, *Uncreative writing. Managing Language in the Digital Age,* (New York: Columbia University Press, 2011).

6. "Kenneth Goldsmith reads poetry at White House Poetry Night." YouTube video, 6:41. "poetryfilmfestival," 12.05.2011. https://www.youtube.com/watch?v=hMSvrIPhA4Y (accessed 29.08.2019).

7. *"Torekes* land and money," Langrangian Republican Association, https://republicoflagrangia.org/2016/08/14/torekes-land-and-money/(accessed 29.08.2019). Note: *Toreke* is a currency used in the Rabot neighborhood in the city of Ghent. This currency is issued by the City to inhabitants who perform certain tasks (such as cleaning the neighborhood) and, in return, people can use this currency to rent a small allotment garden. Since the allotment gardens are located on an abandoned plot of land already owned by the city, the authorities can issue *Torekes* at virtually no cost. Consequently, this local currency allows stimulation of the local economy without increasing the debt of the city.

8. Donna Haraway, *Staying with the Trouble: Making Kin in the Chthulucne*. (Durham: Duke University Press, 2016).

9. "Stijn Van Dorpe, Life in Proximity to the Arts – A Collage of Thoughts," In Proximity to the Arts, http://in-proximity-to-the-arts.nl/ (accessed 29.08.2019). Note: For me, 'third spaces' arise through relational actions and find their place between people. They are in-between spaces which sojourn in between the institutional art space and other places created by society. As such, they attempt to break through the classification of territories, which is a manner to decide who can speak about what. I assign them the ability to replace and to widen the perspective on what is and what isn't seen and heard. Nevertheless, 'third spaces' are strongly connected to the museum because they turn existing places and situations into spaces for showing. But contrary to the institutional, 'neutral' white cube, which historically hides its ideological framework, intervening through 'third spaces' always means launching a consciously ideological process that makes forms of equality tangible and brings them into practice. When we approach 'third spaces' as an organic collective of many similar practices that generate alternative social spaces for the art, they can shift the ecology of the art field as a step to shift society.

10. "The Golden Apartment. Ongoing," Over Piloot.co, http://piloot.co/current/golden-apartment-lotte-geeven/ (accessed 29.08.2019) and "Meer dan object,"

Issuu, pp. 91 – 94, https://issuu.com/vlaamsbouwmeester/docs/kio_web (accessed 08.09.2019).
11. "Een nieuw leven voor de Sint-Jozefkerk," Gent: Bruggen naar Rabot, https://stad.gent/bruggen-naar-rabot/deelprojecten-bruggen-naar-rabot/een-nieuw-leven-voor-de-sint-jozefkerk (accessed 29.08.2019).
12. Tomoko Sauvage, "Magical stones, echoes, and music for animals and atmosphere: an interview with Akio Suzuki," in *The Middle Matter. Sound as Interstice,* eds. Julia Eckhardt, Caroline Profanter, Henry Andersen (Brussel: Umland, 2019), 29.
13. Wikipedia. 2019. "Six Characters in search of an Author." *https://en.wikipedia.org/wiki/Six_Characters_in_Search_of_an_Author (accessed 29.08.2019).* Note: *Six Characters in Search of an Author (Sei personaggi in cerca d'autore)* is a play by Luigi Pirandello, written and first performed in 1921. It is an absurdist meta-theatrical play about the relationship among authors, their characters, and theatre practitioners.
14. Wim Cuyvers, *'Nouvelle. Ecole. Architecture',* C.A.R.A. conference, ULB, Brussels, 17.10.2013.
15. Wikipedia. 2019. "Utopia." https://en.wikipedia.org/wiki/Utopia_%28book%29 (accessed 29.08.2019). Note: Thomas Moore, *Libellus vere aureus, nec minus salutaris quam festivus, de optimo rei publicae statu deque nova insula Utopia,* 1516. The title translates as: "A truly golden little book, no less beneficial than entertaining, of a republic's best state and of the new island Utopia." 'Utopia' is derived from the Greek. The name literally means "nowhere", emphasizing its fictionality.
16. "Philippe Quesne, Crash park. La vie d'une île," Kaaitheater, https://www.kaaitheater.be/fr/agenda/crash-park (accessed 29.08.2019).
17. "Virgina Dwan, a Jet Age Medici, Gets Her Due," The New York Times, https://www.nytimes.com/2016/09/18/arts/design/virginia-dwan-a-jet-age-medici-gets-her-due.html (accessed 29.08.2019). Note: Virginia Dwan inherited her wealth from her grandfather who had a role in founding the Minnesota Mining and Manufacturing Company—better known as 3M.
18. Gustave Flaubert, *Bouvard et Pécuchet,* (Paris: Editions Gallimard, 1881). 23.
19. "Over Aclagro," Aclagro, http://www.aclagro.be/nl (accessed 29.08.2019). Note: As a contractor, Aclagro nv focuses on a number of core activities: infrastructure, soil remediation and water treatment, demolition, soil cleaning, and brownfield. A full vertical integration combined with an extensive machine park and the available human capital make the group unique in its strength, speed, and quality of execution.
20. "Over Oryx," Oryx, http://www.oryx-projects.be/index.html (accessed 29.08.2019). Note: Oryx Projects nv is a Belgian

project developer, which together with a.o. Aclagro nv, AC Materials nv, etc. is part of the Square Group. On 1 January 2014, it was decided to bundle all competencies in project development into the separate entity Oryx Projects nv. The name 'Oryx' is derived from an elegant, powerful, intelligent, and resilient African antelope species that manages to survive the extreme conditions of the desert, a metaphor that speaks for the ever-changing world of project development.

21. "Over Tondelier," https://www.tondelier.be/nl/over-tondelier (accessed 29.08.2019).

22. "Over Injectis," Injectis, https://www.injectis.com/nl/over-ons (accessed 29.08.2019). Note: Injectis bvba is a young and dynamic company that originated in 2017 around the innovative Spin® injection technology. With this, Injectis bvba focuses its efforts on performing high-quality direct injections of all kinds of products for in-situ soil remediation. The scope of products to be injected ranges from chemical oxidants, acids, bases and salts to all sorts of carbon sources for stimulation of biological degradation such as lactate, molasses, emulsified vegetable oils, etc. Injectis bvba itself is not a soil remediation contractor, but works mainly on behalf of certified soil remediators.

23. "Bedrijfsnetwerk Tondelier Development nv," Staatsbladmonitor, https://www.staatsbladmonitor.be/bedrijfsnetwerk.html?ondernemingsnummer=0843882479 (accessed 29.08.2019).

24. "Bedrijfsnetwerk Koramic Real Estate nv," Staatsbladmonitor, https://www.staatsbladmonitor.be/bedrijfsnetwerk.html?ondernemingsnummer=0405371710 (accessed 29.08.2019).

25. Pier Vittorio Aureli, *Less is enough. On architecture and asceticism,* (Moscow: Strelka Press, 2013). Note: 'Less is more' goes the modernist dictum. But is it? In an age in which we are endlessly urged to do "more with less," can we still romanticize the pretensions of minimalism? For Pier Vittorio Aureli, the return of "austerity chic" is a perversion of what ought to be a meaningful way of life. Charting the rise of asceticism in early Christianity and its institutionalization with the medieval monasteries, Aureli examines how the basic unit of the reclusive life—the monk's cell—becomes the foundation of private property. And from there, he argues, it all starts to go wrong. By late capitalism, asceticism had been utterly aestheticized. It manifests itself as monasteries inspired by Calvin Klein stores, in the monkish lifestyle of Steve Jobs and Apple's aura of restraint. Amid all the hypocrisy, it must still be possible to reprise the idea of "less" as a radical alternative, as the first step to living the life examined.

26. Wikipedia. 2019. "Tar." https://en.wikipedia.org/wiki/Tar (accessed 29.08.2019). Note: Tar is a dark brown or black viscous liquid of hydrocarbons and free carbon, obtained from a wide variety of organic materials through destructive distillation. Tar can be produced from coal, wood, petroleum, or peat. Production and trade in pine-derived tar was a major contributor in the economies of Northern Europe and Colonial America. Its main use was in preserving wooden sailing vessels against rot. The largest user was the Royal Navy of the United Kingdom. Demand for tar declined with the advent of iron and steel ships. Tar-like products can also be produced from other forms of organic matter, such as peat. Mineral products resembling tar can be produced from fossil hydrocarbons, such as petroleum. Coal tar is produced from coal as a byproduct of coke production.

Mapping The Set

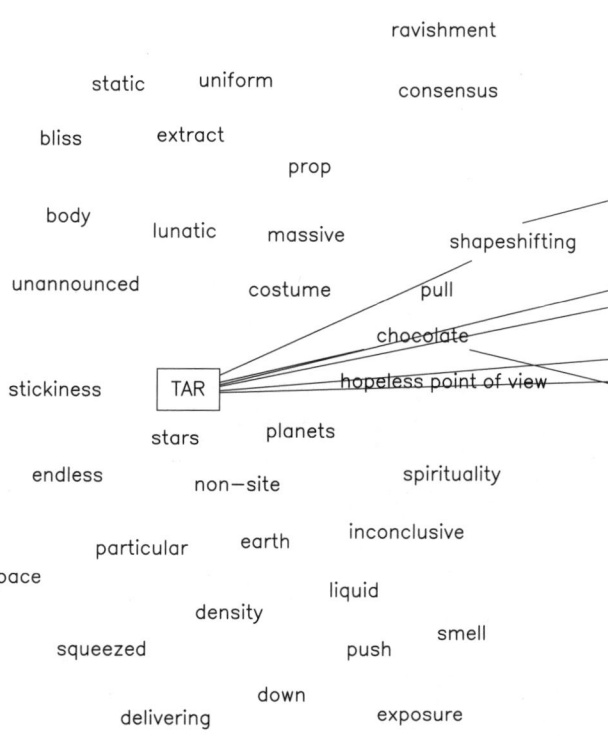

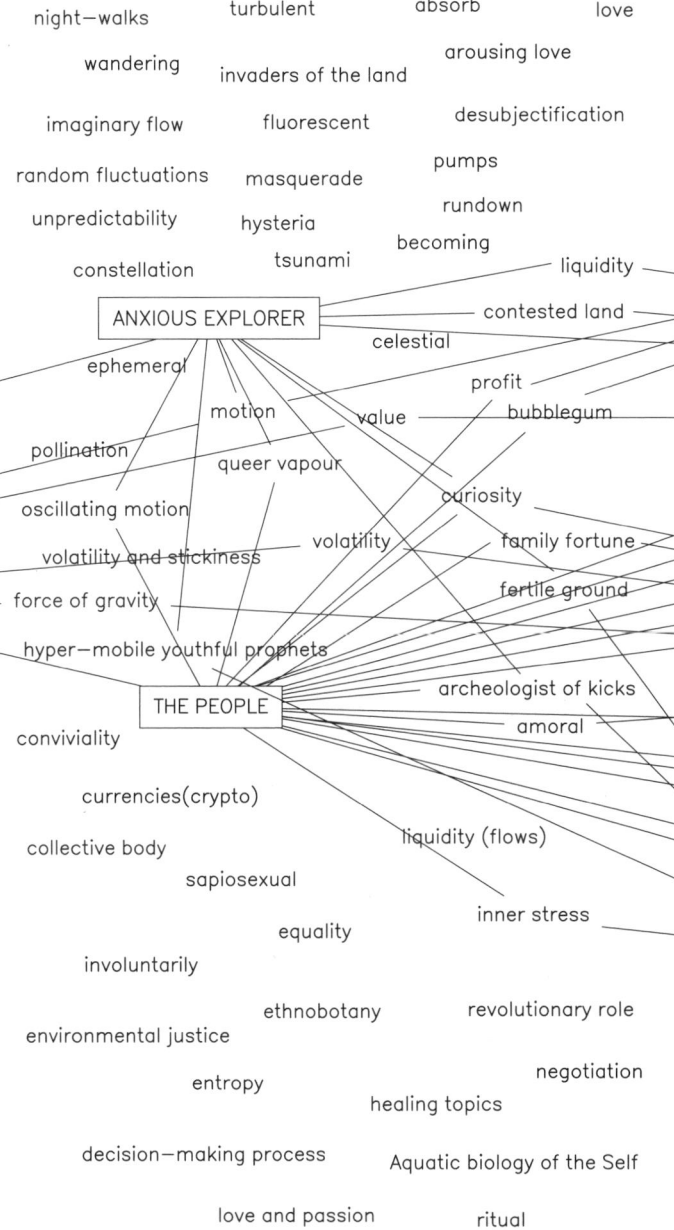

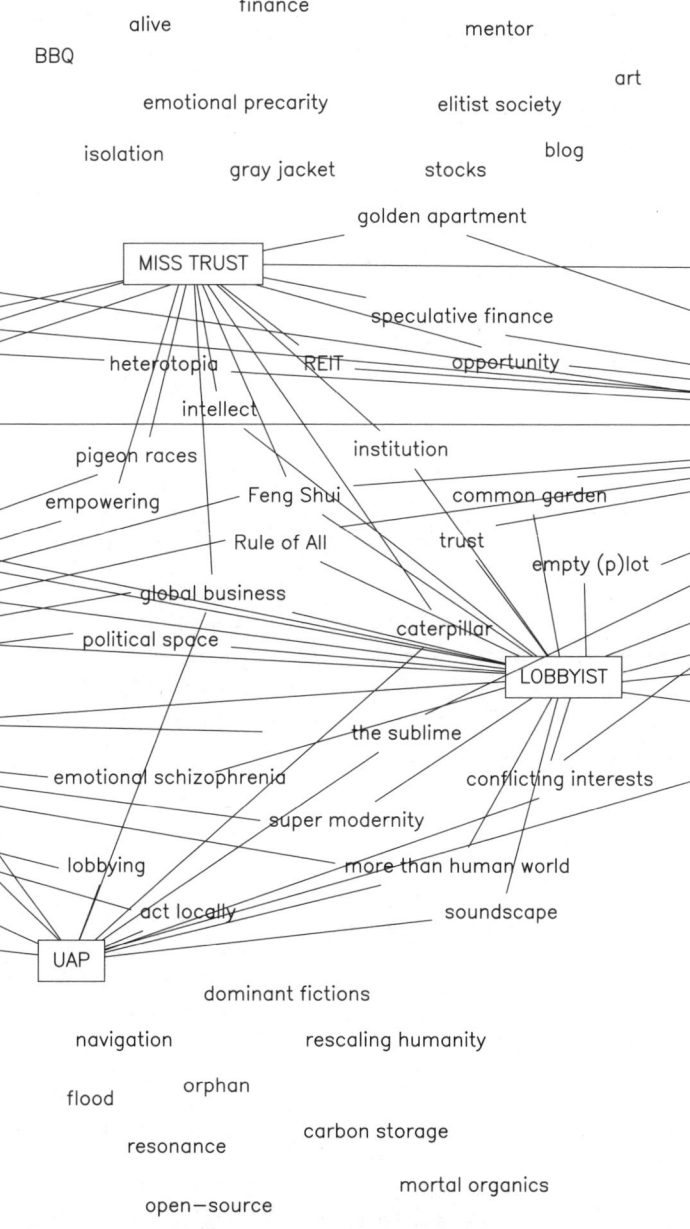

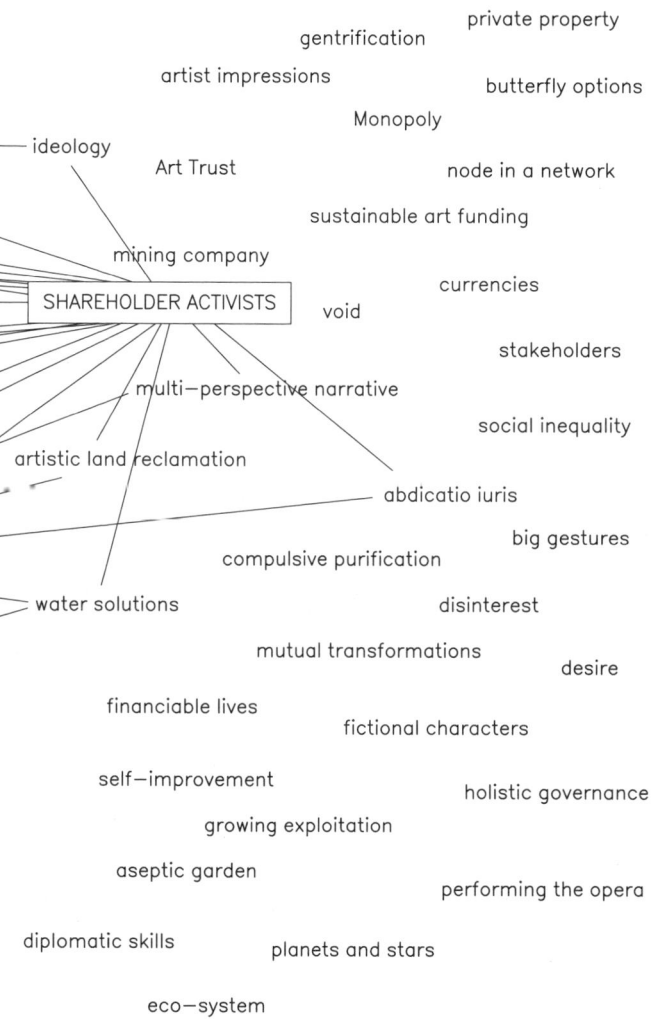

Characters

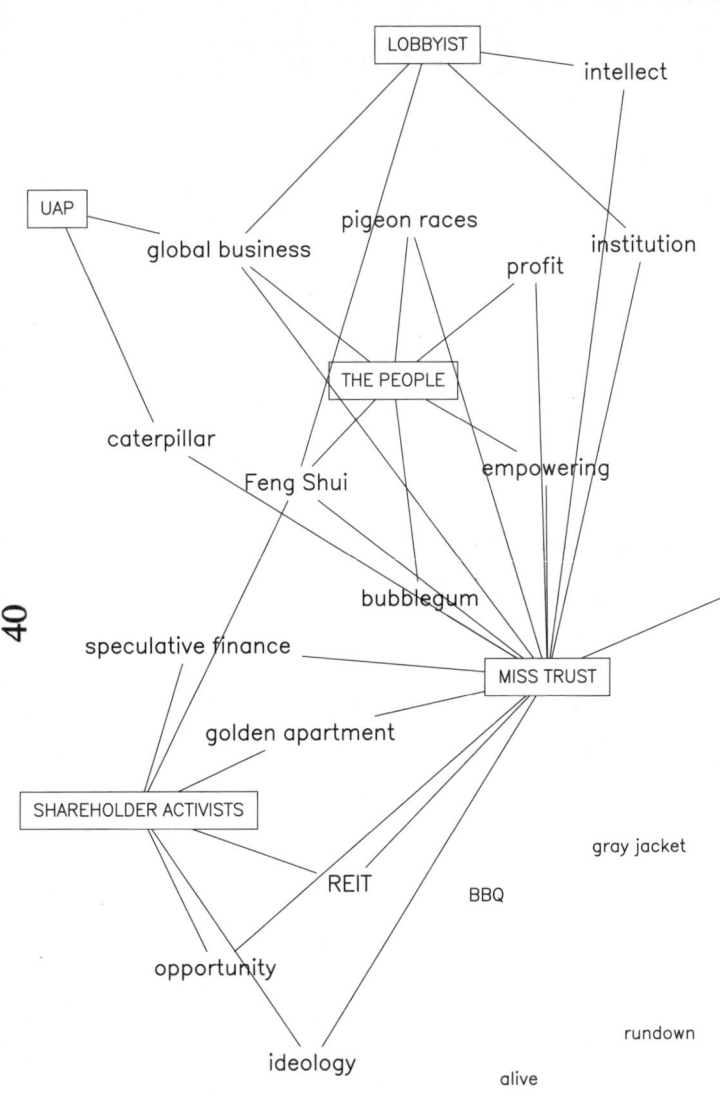

Miss Trust

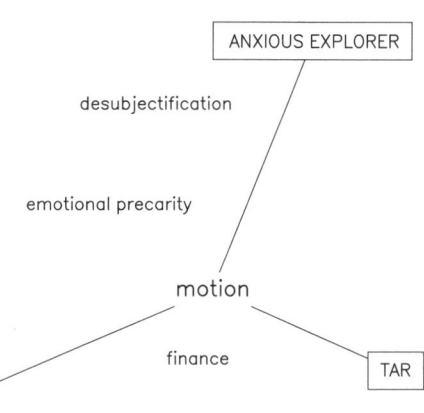

ANXIOUS EXPLORER

desubjectification

emotional precarity

motion

finance   TAR

stocks

elitist society

love

mentor

isolation

Miss Trust, born in London as Tessa Lisbeth Müller-Trust, is half-British, half-German. Her father Carl Harold Trust was the founder and CEO of Trust – Funds and Finance Analysis, based in London, Frankfurt, Hong Kong and New York. He and his wife Elisabeth died in a tragic accident in January 2016. Their private helicopter collided with an unidentified aircraft, which turned their skiing trip in the Italian Alps into a nightmare.[1] Tessa became an orphan at the age of twenty-one. She and her older brother inherited the family's fortune, with real estate in England, Australia, Belgium, Switzerland and Panama. The majority of the company's shares is now owned by the siblings, who both had been groomed to take over the Trust management—her brother, the Asian and American markets, and Tessa, the European, including the mining company 3M. The two of them have a difficult relationship and communicate only via their consultants, and only about business.

Miss Trust is currently pursuing a Master's degree in finance analysis in London.[2] After the 2016 Brexit referendum,[3] she decided to move to Belgium because she believes in the values of a united Europe more than in a splintered outdated illusionary empire, ruled by an old-fashioned monarchy and a conservative parliament. Her current address is *The Golden Apartment* at the top of the only block which has yet been built at Tondelier, as if she was actually performing an artist impression for future shareholder activists.

Henry Passé-Ville (Lobbyist From The Grave) was a very close friend to Carl and Elisabeth and started an intimate affair with Tessa when she was 'barely' mature. Tessa was a diagnosed *sapiosexual*, which explains her hunger for intellectuals often much older than her.[4] Although her relationship with Henry was once profound, open, and desubjectified, it is now fading. Tessa is growing out of her role as a scholar, and her feelings have begun to stagnate. Now platonic, the relationship is kept alive only for pity and nostalgia. His professional expertise is exhausted, and she is more and more morally disgusted by Henry's transformation from a successful expert to an old, sick, and confused man. Tessa knows what to do when his cancer comes back. As his trustee, she signs the papers authorizing his euthanasia. Only she knows the hiding place of the drugs he collected throughout his last chemotherapy. *Mariners Apartment Complex* is a song which connects them deeply and describes their precarious situation, since Lana Del Rey gave a private concert at a BBQ in *The Golden Apartment*.

Her favorite color is Taupe Green.[5] She wears jumpsuits which are especially tailored for her, combined with a jacket by her favourite designer, The Trendy People. The cloth both camouflages her in a sort of uniform, and blends her with The People. The color of her character moves in the grey zones of emotional and moral precarity. Her appearance is that of a ginger-haired, attractive young woman, somewhere between lady-chic, the street-style of the Spanish singer Rosalía, the wilderness and intellect of the American creative writer and director Lena Dunham, and the melancholy of Margot Tannenbaum.[6] Because of this, she recently signed a contract with The Trendy People to be their Instagram influencer. She is about to set up a concept store on the Tondelier site in the centre of *The Golden Apartment*—the perfect spot to promote the ideology of The Trendy People whenever she hosts a BBQ.

Miss Trust made her first million when she was twelve. She has been a member of the *British Royal Pigeon Racing Association* since she was eight years old.[7] Her grandmother bred German messenger pigeons as an exclusive sport and money machine, which later financed the Trust agency. Miss Trust, due to extreme exposure to pigeon excrement, developed an allergy, which turned into a cleaning neurosis. The precaution measures to avoid the allergic reaction created a compulsive routine of cleansing, often starting with a dive into fresh water streams.

Miss Trust usually chews pink bubble gum. She once told her consultant, the UAP, that it helps her think about how she might one day break the elitist, Western-centered bubble that she lives in.[8] From the outside, Miss Trust is an explosive combination of a curious and experimental vamp, while from the inside, she is seriously doubting what the values of the society she grew up in are. Therefore she is considering refusing her heritage. She wants to transform something, even if this was just to move Tar.

In January 2018 at a Trust memorial ceremony BBQ for her dead parents, Miss Trust got to know the UAP, a fascinating elegant female dandy, by talking about invasive vertebrates with her. Inspired by her visionary and super modern Feng Shui adaptations and her interest in pigeons, she replaced her old consultant with the UAP to develop a 'water dynamic' strategy for Tondelier. They became friends quickly and worked on her cleaning obsession in the *Aquatic Biology of the Self* sessions. The UAP gradually introduced her to the quality of energetic well-being, and to the beneficial role of land art. When she finds out about the UAP's influence and long history of corruption, her understanding of the word 'trust' changes.

Miss Trust decides to do another Master's program, this time in the arts, which would turn out to trigger a significant mind shift for her. Tessa starts writing about her professional experiences and the circle she had been born into as an open-source of financial insights. She publishes essays on her blog as Miss Trust. The finance and business world is all eyes and ears thanks to her clever observations and her contacts in both social spheres. She is aware of the ambiguous role that art plays in the world of finance. By combining her expertise in finance and her newfound experience in art, she finds her research topic: *Alternative Finance Methods for Artistic Research and its Execution*.

The mutual Shareholder Activists' REIT (real estate investment trust) is, in fact, the first attempt to use real estate as a sustainable art funding resource. Together with the Shareholder Activists and 3M she will override the Tondelier plot with an artistic transformation of the omnipresent material: tar.

Miss Trust is a multiple winner of the *World Messenger Pigeon Championship*. She met The Anxious Explorer, an exotic young female biology expert in endemic species, when the trophy of her last race was delivered at her doorstep. The award was alive: an Emirate-bred pigeon. Sadly, the pigeon was flattened into the sun-heated tar by one of the 3M mining caterpillars. The Anxious Explorer offered to provide a replacement. Tessa was taken by the smart young woman, and invited her up to play her favourite parlour game: Monopoly. Ever since, the exchange pigeons have been carrying encyclopaedic notes as an encrypted language to plot against the system they live in.

1. "Crash zwischen Heli und Kleinflugzeug. Italien: Pfaffenhausener Unternehmer unter den Opfern," Kurierverlag Mindelheim, https://www.kurierverlag.de/mindelheim/italien-pfaffen hausener-unternehmer-unter-opfern-11584374.html (accessed 29.01.2019).
2. "Master in Financial Analysis," London Edu, https://www.london. edu/masters-degrees/masters-in-financial-analysis (accessed 26.08.2019).
3. "Der Brexit und die britische Sonderrolle in der EU," Bundeszentrale für politische Bildung, https://www.bpb.de/ internationales/europa/brexit/ (accessed 12.08.2019).
4. D. Raab, "Sapiosexuality: What Attracts You to a Sexual Partner?," https://www.psychologytoday.com/intl/blog/the-empowerment-diary/201408/sapiosexuality-what-attracts-you-sexual-partner (accessed 26.08.2019)
5. Pantone 5645
6. The Royal Tannenbaums. Directed by Wes Anderson. (U.S. Customs House Film, 2001, New York, USA).
7. Royal Pigeon Racing Association, https://www.rpra.org/about-rpra/ (accessed 26.08.2019)
8. *The Bubblegum* is an experimental singing technique developed during the rehearsals for *The Orphans of Tar*. The character is put at a distance first, and then gets abruptly prioritized when the bubble unexpectedly bursts.

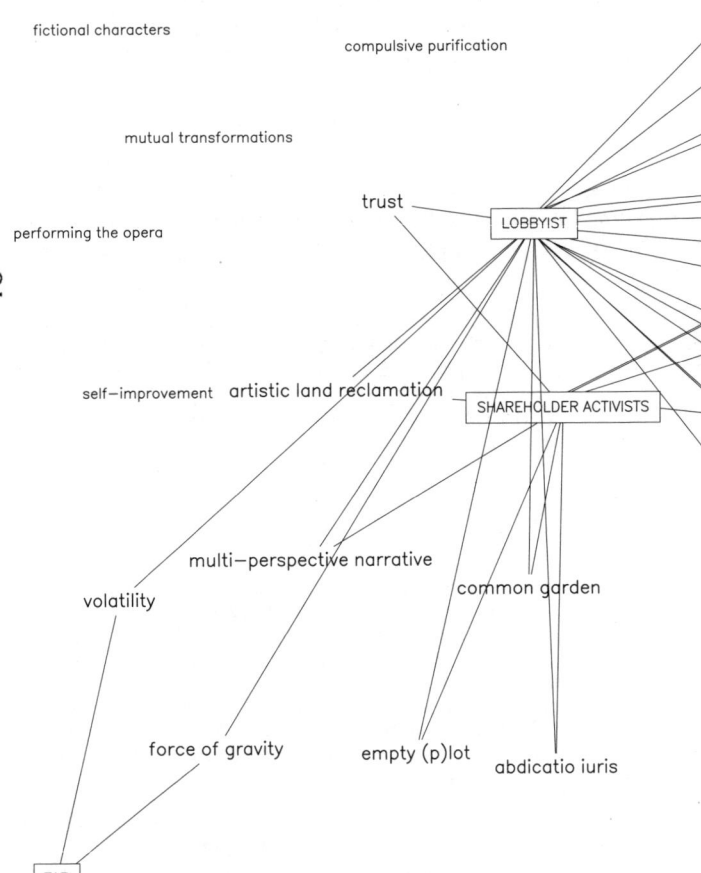

Henry Passé-Ville (Canada, 1955), moves back to Belgium in 2016, after having worked at the University of Amsterdam as a former lobbyist. He was part of the research project *Corporate Europe 2004 – Brussels,* which resulted in an online publication delivering an overview of lobbying in Brussels, as well as specific tours highlighting the lobbying powers in different sectors—finance, carbon and agribusiness.[1/2] In an article that he issued as a postdoctoral fellow in summer 2016, he describes gentrification as "a process of mutual transformations, spatially highly differentiated but impossible to place within any moral and ethical framework." Reading his own statement, Henry collapses under the stress that has been accumulating inside him for many years, due to being squeezed between his personal reflections on his experiences and the realities surrounding him. What do these publications become once they start to influence institutionalized structures? At that point, he receives an invitation for an assistant teaching position from an UAP (Undisciplined Advanced Practitioner) friend—an artist and scholar at the KU Leuven who developed an inconclusive thesis entitled *Advanced Practices for Contested Land/s* that was deemed worthy of continuing, but not yet fit to be defended. Attracted by the fact that he would work in the shadows for a while, Henry has double feelings. He is absolutely relieved that direct attention on his personal thoughts would cease. At the same time, however, he feels defeated, realizing that his capacities never seem to find fertile grounds in which to contribute positively.

      Part of his UAP-friend's advanced practice involves co-owning an apartment within the complex of the Tondelier site in Ghent, where Henry is invited to stay for the first two years after his move to Belgium.[3] His flatmate is the daughter of a CEO of Trust-COOP, a 'greenhouse' for finance and corporate value,[4] Tessa

Müller-Trust (to be found on Instagram as #MissTrust). In her, Henry finds an interesting mix of an open-minded master-student and a highly spoiled child with a challenging intellect—characteristics he is simultaneously attracted to and extremely repelled by. Nevertheless, inspired by his emotional schizophrenia, and influenced by his UAP-friend's artistic sense, Henry decides to spend much of his time writing. Despite not having had any previous experience, he turns out to be an enthusiastic essayist. This is made apparent on Miss Trust's blog after she convinces Henry to collaborate on her latest project, *Emotional Precarities in times of massive technification*.

On the blog, Henry writes: "(…) Indeed, I think a lobbyist is an activist who seeks to persuade members of the government to enact legislation that would benefit their group. The lobbying profession is a legitimate and integral part of our democratic political process that is not very well understood in general. While most people think of lobbyists only as paid professionals, there are also many volunteer lobbyists. Anyone who petitions the government or contacts their member of Parliament to voice an opinion is functioning as a lobbyist. Lobbying is a regulated industry (…) in good times, but runs out of hand when stakes and density of conflicting interests are high. (…).[5] The Treaty of Lisbon introduced a new dimension of lobbying at the European level that is different from most national lobbying. At the national level, lobbying is more a matter of personal and informal relations between the officials of national authorities, but at the European Union level, lobbying is increasingly a part of the political decision-making process and thus part of the legislative process (…).[6] What remains unexplored entirely, though, is the emotional capacity of those who lobby. After years of struggle, I have come to the understanding that I may be completely unsuitable. What has always fueled my drive to represent interests is born out of a paradox: I couldn't care less, and, at the same time, I live for things as if it were my last day on earth. This affects me and my surroundings greatly on an energetic level. While it gives a dynamic to negotiations, it also produces enduring frustration on my side. The latter must have to do with the fact that, doing the job I do, I think that it is disgusting to even imagine having power over others. My only aim is to empower others. It freaks me out that no one seems to be interested in making this differentiation—with the exception for some experimental artists and bold philosophers."

During the last gathering, Henry's students suggest that he should get back into business. He should just keep doing what he has done all his life, but now without any hope. From this radical point of view, he should work with both the wisdom he gained out of his despair and the sense for celebration that he seems not to have lost. Henry, agreeing to play his role in what is for him a refreshing world of young people, knows all too well that those in power do not just physically meet. Where he does see an opportunity is in arranging absolutely nothing at all. This constitutes a new take on his former strategic agenda.

He feels a Woyzeck-like calling from the site itself, an urge to "listen to the grass".[7] The Set speaks to him at night: "Look where those in power are and know that it's just their position that makes them rule!" With the discipline he is born with, he starts making early morning and late night walks. Like an ornithologist, he walks at a very slow and regular pace, just listening and noting down all he hears. During his second walk he *hears* and eventually meets the Anxious Explorer, a sleepless artistic researcher and—as it turns out— a close friend of Miss Trust. The two will make many of the slow walks together. One of them bears a next milestone in Henry's new career: the appearance of Tar during a full moon night walk. Seated next to the Anxious Explorer on a little hill overseeing the rest of the caterpillar-filled site, a black glitter emerges from the soil. From that moment on, Tar will obsess his thoughts. He sees it everywhere and all the time. In its most liquid as well as most manifested form of roads and highways, Tar becomes omnipresent for Henry and installs itself for him as a metaphor for the ever-flowing and sticking currencies that make lives financeable. This connects him—against his will—to the Shareholder Activists, playing a major, but not often visible, role in how money rules decision making processes. For Henry, they are the reason to develop a deeply grounded despair which is caused not so much by people who know how to deal with money but by the opposite species: those who are ignorant—for whatever reasons—about the dynamics that control what gets realized and what is not.

    Henry is, therefore, joining The People—a community of citizens that gather around an artist who seems to look at the world with a similar skepticism and love than he does. At moments, he even dreams of him as a ghostlike ally that he suspects is representing the only possible form of existence: being dead and alive at the same time.

1. "Transparency of lobbying at EU level." Europarlement, http://www.europarl.europa.eu/RegData/etudes/BRIE/2015/572803/EPRS_BRI(2015)572803_EN.pdf (accessed 02.08.2019).
2. Wikipedia. 2019. "European Union lobbying." https://en.wikipedia.org/wiki/European_Union_lobbying (accessed 02.08.2019).
3. "Tondelier, dat is een nieuwbouwproject in Gent, enig in zijn soort in Europa." https://www.tondelier.be/nl/ (accessed 02.08.2019).
4. "Over Oryx," Oryx, http://www.oryx-projects.be/index.html (accessed 29.08.2019). Note: ORYX is committed to achieving continuously solid growth in finance and corporate value.
5. "What is a lobbyist?" https://www.tripsavvy.com/faqs-about-lobbying-1039165 (accessed 14.07.2019).
6. Wikipedia. 2019. "European Union lobbying." https://en.wikipedia.org/wiki/European_Union_lobbying (accessed 02.08.2019).
7. Georg Büchner's 'Woyzeck', a stage play first published in 1879, presents with its protagonist an archetype of human suffering and resulting madness. Woyzeck's mental health is breaking down and he begins to hallucinate and receives messages from e.g. the growing grass, the running water etc.

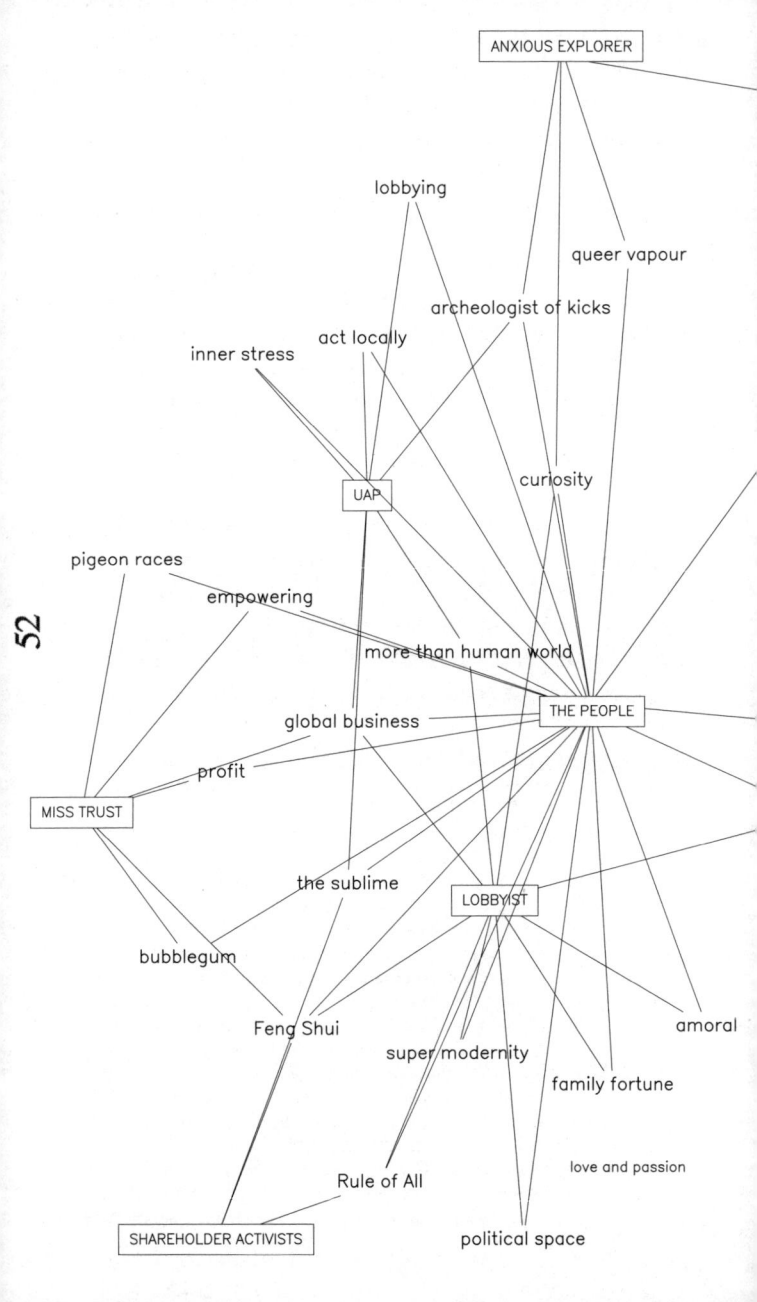

The People

oscillating motion

conviviality

environmental justice

collective body

equality

hopeless point of view

currencies(crypto)

liquidity (flows)

emotional schizophrenia

involuntarily

chocolate

sapiosexual

TAR

volatility and stickiness

spirituality

The People alternately show up in different shapes. They appear first of all as The People, an ephemeral smoky haze, as a ghost representing its ideological core. Sideways, they emerge as The Trendy People, a grey jacket brand inspired by the working class uniform. And finally they appear as The People of Tondelier, a collective body deeply influenced by ideological values and currently gathered around an artist. Another form of The People could become manifest when, in performing the opera, the real people of the Tondelier become co-authors by producing their noise as part of the choir.

    The ghostlike character is portrayed as a fuzzy after-image of an old white man with a white beard.[1] A phantom that is haunting many parts of the earth, but in the last decennia was discredited by many of his earlier fervent disciples. That's why the character is looking for new ways to exert his influence. He's convinced that this is very necessary today. Nonetheless, he became a figure of doubt, dreaming at night about a transformation in queer vapour.[2] Following his desires in the course of the play, the personal pronoun will shift to a 'she'.

    Notwithstanding her human traits leading to an identity crisis, it is important to point out that she (The People), in essence, always remains a speck with one core value. Therefore, she is in many ways the counterpart to the Anxious Explorer with her distracted nature. They are not central characters, although they both influence the course of things in specific ways. Where the Anxious Explorer sets the plot in motion without any agenda (and for sure not a political one), The People change and interfere with the plot from an extremely radical political and very conscious effort. The People has nothing less in mind than the 'Rule of All' and she assures us that there's nothing to negotiate! She is therefore the embodiment of the most radical form of democracy. 'Democracy' is the manifestation of the aspiration that all the people of a region (in optimum condition of the whole planet), and 'nothing' else, order and regulate their common life together.[3]

This is highly political because it will never become a reality by itself. In other words, this value is not a natural condition. According to The People, it is of great importance to realize that this value, if it can exist, needs to be taken serious and fought for, time and again.[4] She's dealing here with a deeply rooted archaic and steadfast concept called 'ideology'. She's very aware of that. She even often gets blamed for it. Nevertheless, and without a bit of jealousy, she adores the flourishing hyper-mobile youthful prophets with their many-armed tentacles, great virtuosity, and, in some cases, complete liquidity who can find access to cunning, handsome, and creative brains.[5] It makes her only more aware of her static position.

A shift in her development came after a conversation she had with the UAP—a good example of such a fluid, creative mind. The UAP not only connects to water, vertebrate animals, plants etc., but also to immaterial creatures. However, it never becomes clear for the audience if this conversation is taking place for real or only in the restless imagination of The People herself. She finds the way the UAP relates to a more-than-human-world—rescaling humanity within a broader eco-system—very appealing. However, she warns of the danger of a naive political worldview when the UAP keeps paraphrasing Bruno Latour's rotation of the political landscape.[6] Which power, which authority, and which hierarchies will take over when the 'Rule of All' evaporates, she asks? At that moment rumours reach the plot that a multitude of people with yellow fluorescent jackets are approaching Tondelier, shouting loudly: "We want our share of the virtually divided cake!" The conversation gets aborted abruptly. Shareholder Activists get seriously worried for the first time.

Inspired by the mobility of people like the UAP, The People want to transform into a virus. This means that she wants to reach a diluted, infinitely multiplied existence. Without denying anything of her essential being, she wants to experiment with all kinds of mutual forms of existence. This has nothing to do with entering into forms of consensus, quite the contrary is true![7] When Miss Trust buys her grey worker's jacket from The Trendy People, we get a taste of such an interfering strategy. Affecting the emotionally precarious state of this young person's mind through an alliance with branding mechanisms, our ghost wants to make tangible and spread her radical democratic values. Whether this will really be successful remains an open question, at least in the course of the opera.

When The People of Tondelier finally enter the plot, we experience the ghost's newest, most artistic and seemingly most efficient mutation. A collective body of a growing number of residents, including the Lobbyist from the Grave, Henry Passé-Ville, comes together on a daily basis on the Tar polluted ground of the Tondelier plot to enact a ritual. They absorb the sounds of the environment—thumping excavators, roaring bulldozers, yammering water pumps, clattering gusts of wind, the call of a lost vertebrate—and enter into a dialogue with this environment through a soundscape of noise. For The People of Tondelier, the soundscape relates to a philosopher's frequent use of the term 'noise' to describe the sound that people who are not heard produce.[8]

This grounding act makes them aware of, and connects them to, the physical things and events around them, including the destructive ones. Their own voices—individually played instruments—dialogue with what surrounds them, in an act of being together apart.[9] They feel like matter amongst other forms of matter. It is a strong experience of equality, a collective gesture they want to make against the advancing exploitation of their living environment and subsequently produced social inequality. They want to perform a powerful act of emancipatory awareness, at the same time arousing love—not the love that quietly blends into daily life, but the moment in which love is the whole world, is amongst all.[10]

The People's noise scares the Shareholder Activists. For them it presents a disturbing mental annunciation of the bodies of the residents to act more powerfully in the near future. An introïtus to what will come.

1. Wikipedia. 2019. "Karl Marx." https://nl.wikipedia.org/wiki/Karl_Marx#/media/Bestand:Karl_Marx_001.jpg (accessed 29.08.2019).
2. Referring to the influence of feminist and queer theory on contemporary Marxist thinking. Queer Marxists have welcomed the rise of intersectional analysis and focused on trans struggles as cutting-edge. For example: Drucker Peter, "Queer Marxism". http://www.historicalmaterialism.org/reading-guides/queer-marxism-peter-drucker (accessed 11.09. 2019).
3. Wendy Brown, *Undoing the Demos. Neoliberalism's Stealth Revolution* (New York: Zone Books, 2015), 202.
4. Jacques Rancière, *La Haine de la Democratie,* (Paris: Fabrique éditions, 2005).
5. Referring to a wide range of contemporary adventurous scientists often crossing disciplines (e.g. Haraway Donna and Baricco Alessandro)
6. Bruno Latour, *Waar kunnen we landen?* (Amsterdam: Octavo, 2018).
7. Chantal Mouffe, On the Political (London: Routledge, 2005). Note: Referring to the importance of dissensus (agonistic politics).
8. Jacques Rancière, *Grensganger tussen disciplines. Interview met Jacques Rancière* (Amsterdam: Valiz, 2007).
9. Jacques Rancière, *The Emancipated Spectator* (London: Verso, 2009), 59. Note: 'Being 'together apart' creates a paradoxical combination of 'distance and intimacy' which, according to Jacques Rancière, lies at the heart of politics.
10. "Filosoof Alain Badiou: "Zoek een weg die de wereld verandert", by van Verschuer Nynke, NRC handelsblad, July 26, 2019. https://www.nrc.nl/nieuws/2019/07/26/filosoof-alain-badiou-zoek-een-weg-die-de-wereld-verandert-a3968340?fbclid=IwAR2KKYDg0qY09Nc_DlTggiWc5Mz9AbCV93X45Z8QajQtp71VcmqcdIVdxog (accessed 29.08.2019)

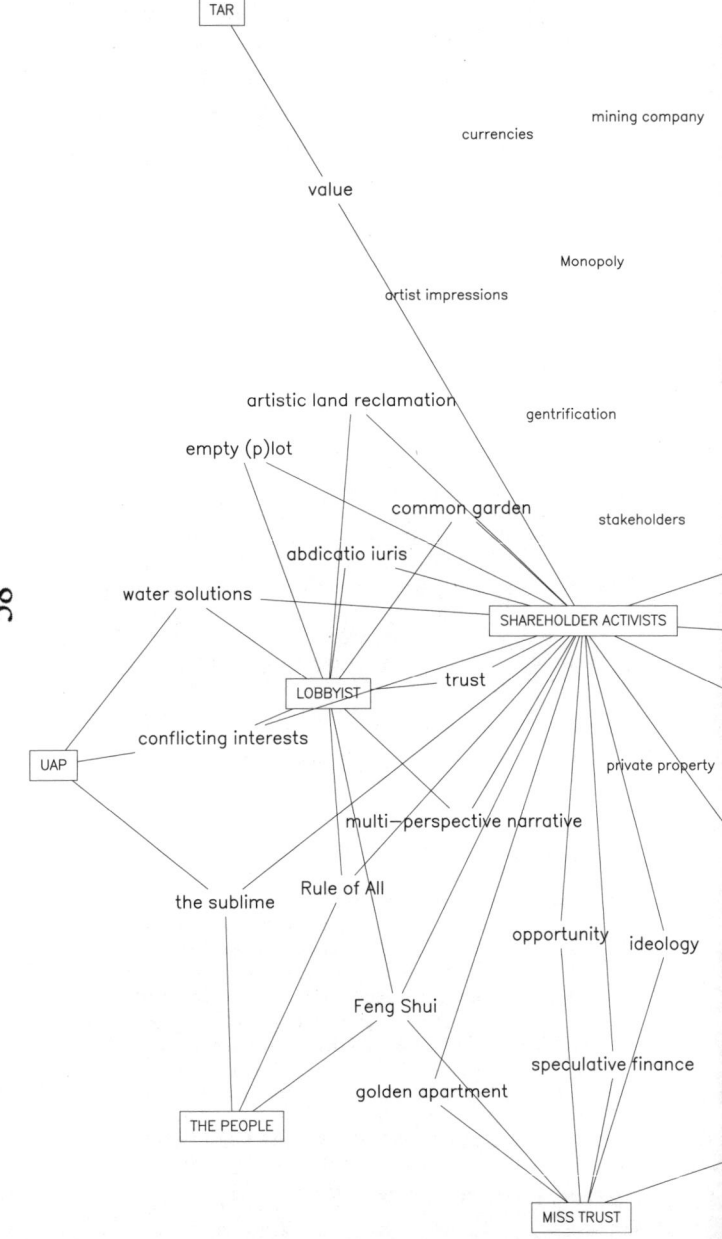

Shareholder Activists

covenant

butterfly options

Art Trust

social inequality

liquidity

contested land

ANXIOUS EXPLORER

heterotopia   node in a network

sustainable art funding

void

REIT

The Shareholder Activists are a multifaceted fictional character. They can act locally, yet they have a global reach. They look like complex creatures with endless tentacles; they are always shapeshifting, always investigating new opportunities. The actions of this multitude could be thought of as akin to the Lobbyist's, except that these creatures are working and pushing from the inside. Their networks are extensive. Pushing management is mostly for their own profit, as the changes they can trigger will send share prices up or make for a higher dividend to be paid out. The main businesses they want to affect are real estate, construction, industry, mining, recycling, and finance, but they are also connected in myriad ways to consulting and even to chocolate, which they devour in copious portions.[1]

As private persons, the Shareholder Activists have multiple personality traits. At times, a single person displays several conflicting characteristics. They are mostly geared towards profit and accumulation, but they can also show some surprising humanity, for example by hosting refugees in their apartments. They also enjoy meditation, and look for ascetic conditions to help them focus on their goals. They look for the sublime, which they can sometimes find in art—especially in big gestures made with land, water, and light.

The Shareholder Activists have multiple connections with Miss Trust. They are fearful of her, as they need trust and credit to move forward with their plans. They fear sudden hysteria and credit drying up, which would result in their businesses collapsing.[2] Miss Trust is living in a virtual apartment on the empty plot. *The Golden Apartment* was proposed by an artist. The idea was to divide one apartment into small blocks so The People could invest in the real estate. The People try to claim a piece of the virtually divided apartment, but the Shareholder Activists pressure their managements not to give in to these claims. It will give The People power to decide on what happens to the plot. It will lessen its value, as they will take the place of potential UHNWI's who will see their presence as undesirable.[3] It will decrease the value of the real estate stocks. The managers have to comply with the Shareholder Activists' wishes, as it is their duty to take care of their interests and maximize profits.

However, the Shareholder Activists like the idea of dividing *The Golden Apartment* into tiny virtual cubicles, as these minimal spaces could be used for ascetic exercises. They want to abstract it even more, and together with Miss Trust they set up a REIT (a real estate investment trust).[4] Together with other real estate assets, *The Golden Apartment* is now part of a diversified portfolio. The rent charged for the ascetic exercises brings a liquid flow that pays the dividends for the global investors, but it will also partially flow into an Art Trust that will even bring more value to their venture.

The Art Trust is a plan set up with the assistance of Miss Trust. She owns the mining corporation 3M, and the Shareholder Activists push her to start mining the Tar that is present in great quantities on the empty set of Tondelier.[5] Tar sand mining is a dirty business, but Miss Trust and the Shareholder Activists have the cunning idea to propose an artistic land reclamation plan that will transform the squalid place into a sublime one.

By bringing it into the centre of the city, non-site will become a site. Entropy will be bliss for the vast numbers of tourists visiting it, and the lucky Tondelier residents will have the opportunity to be immersed in art that changes and transforms any instant, like the land, the tar, the water, the wind, and the light it is made with.[6] Miss Trust's heavy equipment will push and pull and extract Tar, which will be put on freight boats and transported via the canal toward the harbour from where it will be exported globally. Part of the Tar will also be used locally to re-stage Robert Smithson's *Asphalt Rundown* from multiple spots on the plot.[7] The aesthetic of the entropic landscape will awe everyone. The Shareholder Activists can already project their visions: the heroic gestures of dinosaur-like machines moving the mountains of dust and tar flowing down in unpredictable forms and directions brings them to ecstacy. They can already see the extremely adaptive, resilient, and intelligent desert creature, the Oryx, roaming about, attracted by the disturbed earth on The Set.[8]

The Shareholder Activists are pushing their recycling companies' CEO's to write a covenant. Tar, dust, stones, dirt, poison, and smell are no longer liabilities, but new commodities (thanks to art's ability to frame things in a different light) and thus have to be noted in the accounting books as 'assets'. Writing the covenant, the Shareholder Activists come into conflict with The People and with the UAP, as they want to govern The Set differently, taking it out of private ownership. They want to reinstate the gardens and re-install the Canal De Lieve on the site as a commons. The People gave the Shareholder Activists the book *Less is Enough,* to which they refer for their plans with The Set.[9] The book describes the early Franciscan Order's decision not to own things, as a way of refusing potential economic value, and thus the possibility of exploiting others. There, the use of things was not understood as a value, but as an act of sharing and living in common. This conception of use was a radical 'abdicatio iuris', the refusal of the individual's right to private property.

For the Shareholder Activists, however, the right to ownership is the beginning and end of everything. Bliss and spirituality for them is individual, and asceticism is a shaping of their will to power. They also remember that the experiment of the Franciscans did not end well, as the Church forced them to renounce it after a juridical dispute. Property became a fundamental social asset. It created an ethical and moral condition, the goal of which was to ensure social control and increase dedication to work.

The Shareholder Activists are panicking about The People and the UAP's radical ideas, and they ask the Lobbyist From The Grave if he can influence the Feng Shui specialist who is operating on The Set. On the one hand, the flows of energy on The Set need to be assessed in a positive way, as this enhances real estate values. On the other hand, the Feng Shui specialist needs to be convinced that returning to an ecological landscape of gardens and water would be nostalgically going back to scenic ideals. No! The dialectic between human action and the place as found, however poisonous and dirty, is far more heroic and aesthetic. And the reclamation of the land through the transformative powers of art will ensure that the new plot takes hold.

In any case, the Shareholder Activists are betting on two options: on the one hand, they manipulate the Anxious Explorer, to see how she can change the minds of The People and the UAP in adopting the new narrative. On the other hand, they file a case with The Set's neighbour, the Palace of Justice, to have The People and the UAP lawfully expelled from The Set, and the plot. They sell to the Anxious Explorer both 'butterfly short' and 'butterfly long' options.[10] In any of the above scenario's playing out, they will be able to turn a substantial profit, leveraging the power of the new narrative and hedging the risk and volatility of conflicting claims to the underlying asset, The Set.

1. "Bedrijfsnetwerk Tondelier Development nv," Staatsbladmonitor, https://www.staatsbladmonitor.be/bedrijfsnetwerk.html?ondernemingsnummer=0843882479 (accessed 29.08.20).
2. Inspired by the character of *Lady Credit* in the work of Daniel Defoe (1660 – 1731).
3. "Ultra High Net Worth Individual (UHNWI)," Investopedia, https://www.investopedia.com/terms/u/ultra-high-net-worth-individuals-uhnwi.asp (accessed 29.08.2019).
4. "REIT," Investopedia, https://www.investopedia.com/terms/r/reit.asp (accessed 29.08.2019). Note: Individual investors can buy shares in commercial real estate portfolios. The REIT leases space and collects rents on the properties, then distributes that income as dividends to shareholders.
5. "Virgina Dwan, a Jet Age Medici, Gets Her Due," The New York Times, https://www.nytimes.com/2016/09/18/arts/design/virginia-dwan-a-jet-age-medici-gets-her-due.html (accessed 29.08.2019). Note: Virginia Dwan inherited her wealth from her grandfather who had a role in founding the Minnesota Mining and Manufacturing Company — better known as 3M.
6. "Site/nonsite," Researchgate, https://www.researchgate.net/publication/232243344_Art_Ecology_Land_Reclamation_Works_of_Artists_Robert_Smithson_Robert_Morris_and_Helen_Mayer_Harrison_and_Newton_Harrison (accessed 29.08.2019). Note: Inspired by the concepts site/nonsite and entropy in the work of land artist Robert Smithson
7. "Asphalt Rundown," Researchgate, https://www.researchgate.net/publication/232243344_Art_Ecology_Land_Reclamation_Works_of_Artists_Robert_Smithson_Robert_Morris_and_Helen_Mayer_Harrison_and_Newton_Harrison (accessed 29.08.2019). Note: Asphalt Rundown was executed by Robert Smithson on the outskirts of Rome in 1969. A truckload of asphalt was dumped down the slope of a flint quarry.
8. "Over Oryx," Oryx, http://www.oryx-projects.be/index.html (accessed 29.08.2019). Note: Inspired by Oryx real estate company developing Tondelier in Ghent. According to their website, their name "Oryx" is derived from an elegant, powerful, intelligent, and resilient African antelope species that manages to survive the extreme conditions of the desert. A metaphor that speaks for the ever-changing world of project development.
9. Pier Vittorio Aureli, *Less is enough. On architecture and asceticism* (Moscow: Strelka Press, 2013).
10. Wikipedia. 2019. "Butterfly." https://en.wikipedia.org/wiki/Butterfly_(options) (accessed 29.08.2019).

Note: In finance, a *butterfly* is a limited risk, non-directional options strategy that is designed to have a high probability of earning a limited profit when the future volatility of the underlying asset is expected to be lower or higher than the implied volatility when long or short respectively.

Tar's First Insertion

THE PLOT AS PERCEIVED IN TAR

Tar shares its chemically organic nature with the other characters, except for The Set—the only other character not bothered by mortality. Because of its paradoxical silence, its absent presence, and its showing up without firm reason or method, Tar is highly conspiracious with the mortal organics. Reconciling the perspective of Tar to mortality would make little sense. On the other hand, Tar couldn't possibly be able to value any of their intentions. The mortal organics attempt for various movements of its body, but it can't recognize the various outcomes. It doesn't matter; time passes and Tar is being removed from the plot. They are playing a game in which Tar has no vested interest. Some of them are playing a game, which makes that others are confined to that game. Tar is in no way the aim of the game. It is one of its currencies. You play by moving Tar. The intention to move Tar, the demand for movement, or fantasies of what Tar could build are of no real importance in this game. Whether or not you're moving Tar, Tar is on the move. Neither voluntarily nor involuntarily. It is being moved. Players are coming and going, according to opportunities, transactions and consequences at hand. The others may recognize some of these elements, but seem to miss out on the rhythm of the game.

Being quite civilized, some mortal organics have chosen tokens to play on their behalf. Now, this is where things get complicated, as it is not always completely clear who these tokens represent. The plot had been covered with a layer of concrete for some time, which sealed the Tar beneath it. The People were very successful in that period. They used vegetable gardens as tokens, but they also entered the plot themselves. They were visible and easy to find. They didn't hide behind their tokens. Eventually this made them very exposed. At some point, the tokens were replaced.

In the end it was impossible for them to retain the role of the protagonist. Nowadays, the mechanical caterpillars and the cargo boats seem to be on good terms. However, the conductors of these tokens have opted for discretion.

Bibliography:
Theo Deutinger, *The Handbook of Tyranny* (Baden: Lars Müller Publishers, 2018), 37 – 52; 79 – 91.

The Set

Because, you see...

I don't seem to be able to make up my mind.

I need agents to manifest myself. I can be anything or nothing, a void, an empty lot where nothing ever happens, nor ever will. Nobody lives everywhere; everybody lives somewhere. Nothing is connected to everything, but everything is connected to something.[1] When you come over, I'll be there as well, shaping the in-between-you.

You could say I have no character, no will of my own, but I would argue that I have many personalities. In fact, I have as many as there are of you, plus all the permutations of you. Even without you noticing, I have changed. Another agent has stepped in. Only you did not yet meet! It will happen, or it won't. It's not up to me. I guess I'm just a node in a network. Or no... not really, I'm not; I seem to be situated a bit lower, a bit deeper. I seem to be whatever is necessary for the network to exist in the first place. You could say that I'm the condition for things to be as they are, or for them to be how they will be. I'm flexible and I will adapt to your desires. Just be expressive!

How did we end up here? You all decided to write an opera—a work. You agreed to define a number of players, and to write down one shared paragraph present in all characters—a paragraph that would envelop one singular node, like in a multi-perspective narrative. And then you didn't.

I'm wondering if the opera could be performed, e.g. in a garden, or in some other kind of metaphorical place, one situated location in which everything would come together. I could go for that. There would be an early morning soundscape of birds, a tsunami sound wave of bird twitter. And there would be the echoes of stones and white noise concerts with people from the surrounding streets whose voices are usually dismissed as meaningless, who would then enter your story as co-writers and, in doing so, redefine the political space as we know it.

Would there still be the smell of Tar? Inescapable, penetrating, nauseating… the antipode of an aseptic garden. A utopia or a non-place? A place that can be closed off expropriating the common garden. A vision worth pursuing or a critical mirror? A fictional character or a concrete shape? Why does it usually have the tendency to coincide with its opposite: a totalitarian state of salvation? Why can it not remain a place where people can find each other, relieved of pressing rules and collective anxieties. There is but one rule: "Nothing is mine here and yet I am involved in everything."[2]

Maybe we could start from an empty lot, a plot that is in a state of becoming, that plays out and could be anywhere, and that could be built in all kinds of different forms? Your opera could play anywhere. It does not need a fixed place. I can be a landscape, prop, costume, sound, smell. I can be a painting. I can be digital. Just a map, yet adamant about changing the story. Both a maker and a destroyer, not reducible to the sum of my parts, but "achieving finite systemic coherence in the face of perturbations within parameters that are themselves responsive to dynamic systemic processes."[3]

I don't forget anything, but I practice oblivion as a virtue. Because you see, I am The Set.

---

1. Thom Van Dooren, *Flight Ways: Life at the Edge of Extinction* (New York: Columbia University Press, 2014), 60.
2. Wim Cuyvers, *'Nouvelle. Ecole. Architecture'*, C.A.R.A. conference, ULB, Brussels, 17.10.2013.
3. Donna Haraway, *Staying with the Trouble* (Durham and London: Duke University Press, 2016), 44.

pollination

night-walks

tsunami

order and disorder

ephemeral

random fluctuations   turbulent

becoming

myriad

ravishment

hyper-mobile youthful prophets   ANXIOUS EXPLORER

pumps

LOBBYIST   fertile ground

hysteria

UAP   curiosity

wandering

absorb

archeologist of kicks   oscillating motion

unpredictability

contested land

THE PEOPLE — queer vapour

liquidity

74

constellation

Anxious Explorer

fluorescent

consensus

masquerade

invaders of the land

imaginary flow

celestial motion — MISS TRUST

arousing love

shapeshifting

TAR

heterotopia

SHAREHOLDER ACTIVISTS

The Anxious Explorer is a small character flying around in the garden.[1] She is constantly oscillating between volatility and stickiness: a tiny point flittering around The Set. Imagine a butterfly kept above the ground by her oversized wings, but glued to curiosities with the heaviness of sugar addiction.

She oversees the space as a constellation of interconnected transversal subjects of curiosity.[2] Yet, she falls in love with each one as if it were the only one. With this deep, yet short, repetitive fantasy of settling, she is always in motion, jumping from flower to flower, driven by colour ravishment.[3] Between light dawdling and survival, her trajectory is made up of ups and downs due to her over-excitement.[4]

The Anxious Explorer is apolitical. She has no agenda, no age, and no sex. She borrows from the clown her impertinence and seeming clumsiness. Also borrowing traits from the love figures[5] Cupid and the Putti, she is not a central character. In fact, she is even a bit anecdotical, external, disparate. She appears in loose moments, half lucid, half dreamy. She belongs to the back of the stage, passing by like a furtive Ninfa.[6] Yet her trajectory, sharp and unpredictable as arrows, often sets the plot in motion, taking unforeseen paths, with the irrational energy of love and passion,[7] and her power of pollination.[8]

She borrows her moving mechanism from butterflies[9] and ice skaters (who spin faster when bringing their arms close to their bodies). She is a cousin of the Pyrallis, those mythological insect-sized dragons from Cyprus that live inside fire and die if they move away from it. Like them, she cannot stand steadiness and coldness, yet she is continuously and contradictorily compelled to pin those sparkling siblings in her glossy sketchbooks.

The Anxious Explorer pursued degrees (none of them completed) in Archaeology, Geology, Chemistry, and Physics in order to acknowledge and cope with the fatal force of gravity which makes everything rest at some point. Indeed, when lying on the ground, she borrows from her uncompleted studies and undisciplined explorations, terms and principles to fly away from, giving shape to immaterial thoughts. She is constantly flipping her wrist to either light the dark paths she undertakes at night, or to navigate on her phone, which she uses like a weird Pokédex.[10] She copies and pastes everything with an absurd encyclopaedic method because she loves the shape things sometimes make when associated with other things, and she enjoys the ecstasy of collecting, but flies instantly away when meaning becomes too fixed. This is why she uses short quotes outside of their usual context: to evoke new perspective and create stroboscopic knowledge.

For instance, she feels porous[11] to the world—an empathic,[12] physical trait she shares with the flooded ground. This personality trait sometimes makes her unaware of her size, capabilities, and effect on others; as she sees no clear boundaries she uses others' words instead of her own.[13] Footnotes could be the only lyrics she sings.

She knows that nothing flies without gravity, so she cuddles what keeps her down. She spends half of her time lying down, listening, and observing things on the ground, compelled to touch.[14][15] When touched in return, she spaces out, overwhelmed by divergences and analogies which she tries to channel to get in motion again and to keep a trajectory. Oops... how did I get there?[16]

She feels the disrupted energy flowing through the painting[17] even though she has this child-like posture that keeps it abstract, distant, and out of focus, much like observing closely the blurry brush strokes of a Tondelier updated version of a *Fête Galante*.[18] Therefore, she explores her mind, the garden, and the text with fluidity and anxiety, vulnerable to external dynamics, like a butterfly facing the wind.

Even though her journey through the garden is quite lonely, curiosity and conviviality are her fuel. She restlessly looks for encounters, hoping her trajectory will make her bump into other characters and produce a joyful moment of "enamoration".[19]

She is constantly in contact with The People through the screen of her phone, but she is alone in the wild. She reads and uses knowledge which The People have accumulated. She therefore situates herself in this heterogeneous, and always in progress, network built strata by strata, substituting the figure of the bearded old man for a shapeshifting face lit by a cold screen light. Recently, surfing on Miss Trust's blog, she saved an article written by 'Henri Passé-Ville' in her "to read later <3" bookmark.

After traveling an immeasurable amount of time in Tondelier, she even became friends with those faceless caterpillars. She cannot resist finding them cute, even though she sees them as disturbing actors in the natural decanting process The Set is undergoing. Isn't that what she herself also does on a small scale as an undergraduate archaeologist?

When digging too much, she meets the Tar for which she has great sympathy (she shares the same exposure to gravity). She tries to focus on its volatility, yet she is disoriented by its toxicity. Recently, during a stroll in the garden, she thought of the principle of inertia,[20] which she wishes to discuss with the Tar.

Besides wandering around, the Anxious Explorer likes to go to the golden salons organized by Miss Trust, her indoor alter-ego.[21] They are always nice occasions to overdress. She loves Miss Trust's soft and caring theatrical aesthetic for hosting and gifts. But even though she enjoys them a lot, she can stand those indoor meetings only with all windows wide-open.

There, they play Monopoly. The square set is a tough frame to stay focused on, but each street of each box she goes through is an open door to distraction. She learns from experiences of others, talking while playing, keeping her hands busy manipulating the tiny hotels.

1. Michel Foucault, "Des espaces autres," Conférence au Cercle d'études architecturales, 14 mars 1967, in *Architecture, Mouvement, Continuité*, no 5 (1984), 46 – 9. Note: the garden would be the oldest example of heterotopia according to Foucault. It is Tondelier, the mind, the group and project we are in, the text…
2. Wikipedia. 2019. "Cabinet of curiosities." https://en.wikipedia.org/wiki/Cabinet_of_curiosities (accessed 29.08.2019). Note: Cabinet of curiosities (in German: Wunderkammer) were notable collections of objects. The term 'cabinet' originally described a room, rather than a piece of furniture. Modern terminology would categorize the objects included as belonging to natural history (sometimes faked), geology, ethnography, archaeology, religious or historical relics, works of art (including cabinet paintings), and antiquities.
3. "The neuroscience of Aesthetics and Art, Anjan Chatterjee." YouTube video, 1:28:55. "George Kalarritis, Clinical Psychologist," 19.12.2016. https://www.youtube.com/watch?v=R-ktej6TGq8 (accessed 29.08.2019). Note: He calls his approach "aesthetic from below". For instance, he connects the common drive for bright colours to the primal need of vitamin C that resulted in gathering fruit in early stages of human evolution.
4. Carrie Lynn Bailey, "Overexcitabilities and Sensitivities: Implications of Dabrowski's Theory of Positive Disintegration for Counseling the Gifted," *Academia*, https://www.academia.edu/967019/Overexcitabilities_and_Sensitivities_Implications_of_Dabrowskis_Theory_of_Positive_Disintegration_for_Counseling_the_Gifted (accessed 29.08.2019). Note: One could say that one who manifests a given form of overexcitability, and especially one who manifests several forms of overexcitability, sees reality in a different, stronger, and more multifaceted manner. Reality, for such an individual, ceases to be indifferent, but affects him deeply and leaves long-lasting impressions. Enhanced excitability is a means for more frequent interactions and a wider range of experiences. (…)
5. Hilde Bouchez, *A Wild Thing, Essays on Things, Nearness and Love*, (Paris: Art Paper Editions, 2017), 85 – 89. Note: According to Hesiod, first there was Khaos, then Came Gaia and Eros. The Orphic Eros is the god of art, the representation of beauty and inspiration. Socrates explains that love comes out of nowhere, as if on wings. It is a turbulent force that takes control of the psyche and the body, but also makes people grow. (…) Eros is located at the centre of all dualities: between the beautiful and the ugly, between good and evil and, of course, between life and death. (…) Love is terribly restless; it cannot wait for its object, and it is very much in need of the longing that comes from separation from the object of desire. Eros and love can only exist between Being and Becoming.

6. Bertrand Prévost, "Direction-dimension: Ninfa et putti," in *Images Re-vues, histoire, anthropologie et théorie de l'art, Hors-série 4*, 2013, https://journals.openedition.org/imagesrevues/2941 (accessed 29.08.2019). Note: We know how Warburg gave figure to what he called "the schizophrenia of Western civilization": by the dialectic of "the ecstatic (manic) nymph on the one hand, and (the) melancholic (depressive) river god on the other". This is, indeed, a polarity, in the Warburgian sense of the term, and not a simple opposition, in that the relationship between the two poles is a deeply dialectical one: one term does not go without the other—the two are always in a relationship of reciprocity. The image of the pendulum or even the oscillatory movement, used by Warburg himself, is particularly eloquent: it is a way of saying that Ninfa and the river god designate the extreme positions of an interval, within which the images are always Ninfa and river god. And if these positions, as formulas of pathos, are embodied in bodily attitudes, it is less necessary to see them as stations (standing/lying down) than as deeper dynamisms: standing/falling, rising/falling. Georges Didi-Huberman masterfully showed this dialectic in his *Ninfa moderna* since what he calls the "decline of Ninfa" is none other than his sovereign depression—a way of signifying something like Ninfa's permanent melancholic transformation into a river god. Further reading: Georges Didi-Huberman, *Ninfa Profunda, Essai sur le drapé-tourmenté* (Paris: Éditions Gallimard, 2017).

7. Roland Barthes, *Fragment d'un discours amoureux*, (Paris: Éditions du Seuil, 1977), 7. Note: *Dis-cursus* is, originally, the action of running here and there; there are comings and goings, "approaches," "intrigues." The lover never ceases to run in his head, to take new steps and to intrigue himself. So, the lover who is prey to his figures struggles in a slightly crazy sport. He prays on himself; like the athlete, he sentences, like the speaker, he is seized, stunned in a role, much like a statue. The face is the lover at work. (…) If there is an "Anxiety" figure, it is because the subject sometimes shouts out (without worrying about the clinical meaning of the word): "I am anxious!", "Angoscia!" sings Callas somewhere. The figure is in a way an opera aria; just as this aria is identified, "remembered," and handled through his incipit. (…) Throughout his life, the figures appear in the subject's head without any order, because they depend each time on chance (inside or outside). To each of these incidents (what "falls" on him), the lover draws from the reserve (the treasure?) figures,

according to the needs, the injunctions, or the pleasures of his imagination. Each figure explodes, vibrates alone, like a sound cut off from any melody, or repeats itself, satiated like the motif of soaring music. There is no logic that binds the figures, that determines their contiguity; the figures are out of syntagm, out of narrative. They are Erinyes; they shake, collide, calm down, return, and move away, without more order than a flight of mosquitoes. The love discourse is not dialectical; it turns into a perpetual calendar, an encyclopaedia of emotional culture (in the lover, something of Bouvard and Pécuchet

8. Wikipedia. 2019. "Flower (video game)." https://en.wikipedia.org/wiki/Flower_(video_game) (accessed 29.08.2019). Note: *Flower* is a video game released in February 2009. *Flower* was primarily intended to arouse positive emotions in the player, rather than to be a challenging and "fun" game. *Flower* is divided into six main levels and one credits level. Each level is represented by a flower in a pot on the windowsill of a city apartment. Upon selecting a flower, the player is taken to the "dream" of that flower. Once inside a level, the player controls the wind as it blows a single flower petal through the air. Changes in the pitch and roll of the floating petal are accomplished by tilting the PlayStation 3 controller. Pressing any button blows the wind harder, which in turn moves the petal faster. The camera generally follows just behind the petal, though it sometimes moves to show a new objective or consequence of the player's actions.

9. Wikipedia. 2019. "Butterfly Effect." https://en.wikipedia.org/wiki/Butterfly_effect (accessed 29.08.2019). Note: In chaos theory, the Butterfly Effect is the sensitive dependence on initial conditions in which a small change in one state of a deterministic nonlinear system can result in large differences in a later state. The term is derived from the metaphorical example of the details of a tornado (the exact time of formation, the exact path taken) being influenced by minor perturbations such as the flapping of the wings of a distant butterfly several weeks earlier. Wikipedia. 2019. "Chaos theory." https://en.wikipedia.org/wiki/Chaos_theory (accessed 29.08.2019). Note: "Chaos … theory discusses self-organization in terms of islands of predictability in a sea of chaotic unpredictability." "The term edge of chaos is used to denote a transition space between order and disorder that is hypothesized to exist within a wide variety of systems. This transition zone between the two regimes is known as the edge of chaos, a region of bounded instability that engenders a constant dynamic interplay between order and disorder. Wikipedia. 2019. "Self-Organization." https://en.wikipedia.org/wiki/Self-organization (accessed 29.08.2019). Note: Self-Organization also called 'spontaneous order' in the social sciences, is a process where some

form of overall order arises from local interactions between parts of an initially disordered system. The process can be spontaneous when sufficient energy is available, not needing control by any external agent. It is often triggered by random fluctuations, and amplified by positive feedback. The resulting organization is wholly decentralized, and distributed over all the components of the system. As such, the organization is typically robust and able to survive or self-repair substantial perturbation.

10. Wikipedia. 2019. "Gameplay of Pokémon." https://en.wikipedia.org/wiki/Gameplay_of_Pokémon#pokédex (accessed 29.08.2019). Note: Pokémon Zukan (lit. "Pokémon Encyclopedia") is an electronic device designed to catalogue and provide information regarding the various species of Pokémon. The name Pokédex is a portmanteau of Pokémon and index. In the video games, whenever a Pokémon is first caught, its height, weight, species type, and a short description will be added to a player's Pokédex. It is a central tool in this game which has, as a baseline "Catch'em all !". Websites gathering data and online fan forums are often called Pokédex.

11. Wikipedia. 2019. "Porosity." https://en.wikipedia.org/wiki/Porosity (accessed 29.08.2019). Note: Porosity or void fraction is a measure of the void (i.e. "empty") spaces in a material. It is a fraction of the volume of voids over the total volume, between 0 and 1, or as a percentage between 0% and 100%. Wikipedia. 2019. "Permeability." https://en.wikipedia.org/wiki/Permeability (accessed 29.08.2019). Note: The permeability of a medium is related to the porosity, but also to the shapes of the pores in the medium and their level of connectedness. In fluid mechanics and in the earth sciences, it is a measure of the ability of a porous material (often, a rock or an unconsolidated material) to allow fluids to pass through it.

12. Wikipedia. 2019. "Empathy." https://en.wikipedia.org/wiki/Empathy (accessed 29.08.2019). Note: The definitions of empathy encompass a broad range of emotional states, including caring for other people and having a desire to help them, experiencing emotions that match another person's emotions, discerning what another person is thinking or feeling, and making less distinct the differences between the self and the other. It can also be understood as blurring the division between oneself and another. Having empathy can include having the understanding that there are many factors that go into decision-making and cognitive thought processes, and that past experiences have an influence on the decision making of today.

13. Kenneth Goldsmith, *Uncreative Writing: Managing Language in the Digital Age,* (Paris: Jean Boite éditions, 2011), 203. Note: No one can dispute that notions so long honored with creativity are under attack, eroded by file sharing, media culture, multiplication of sampling and digital clones. What is the response of writing to this new environment? The challenge of this course will be to summon the strategies of appropriation, cloning, plagiarism, piracy, sampling, and looting as methods of literary composition. (…) We will see how modern notions of chance, protocol, repetition and the aesthetics of boredom intertwine with popular culture to usurp conventional notions of place, time, and identity as they are expressed linguistically.

14. Jean Claude Ameisen, "Ressentir le monde," Université Paris-Diderot, 13.11.2013, Conférence. https://www.canal-u.tv/video/universite_paris_diderot/ressentir_le_monde_jean_claude_ameisen.13789. (accessed 29.08.2019). Note: If our senses open us to the world, they also restrict us from a part of reality. For example, the nectaire, a small region surrounding the place where nectar is found on some flowers that appear white to us, appear coloured to bees, thanks to their sensitivity to the spectrum of ultraviolet light. It is as if an ecosystem was made of living beings that do not perceive the same way, as if there were no more than fragments of a mirror, or different reflections of reality.

15. "The neuroscience of Aesthetics and Art, Anjan Chatterjee." YouTube video, 1:28:55. "George Kalarritis, Clinical Psychologist," 19.12.2016. https://www.youtube.com/watch?v=R-ktej6TGq8 (accessed 29.08.2019). Note: describes neuro-images of people experimenting beauty and discusses a momentum of "spacing out", or disconnecting, and then spacing back in after a flow of diverging images, or a succession of memories opening up and connecting subjectively. Meaning: this short moment of being dropped somewhere else when facing beauty).

16. Wikipedia. 2019. "Serendipity." https://en.wikipedia.org/wiki/Serendipity (accessed 29.08.2019). Note: Serendipity refers to an unplanned, fortunate discovery. Serendipity is a common occurrence throughout the history of product invention and scientific discovery. Serendipity is also seen as a potential design principle for online activities that would present a wide array of information and viewpoints, rather than just re-enforcing a user's opinion.

17. David Freedberg, Vittorio Gales, "Motion, Emotion and Empathy in Aesthetic Experience," in *Trends in Cognitive Sciences,* Vol, 11 No.5, 2007. Note: The painting will move the soul of the beholder if the people represented in it each clearly show the movement of their own soul. We weep with the weeping, laugh with the laughing, and grieve with the grieving. These movements of the soul are expressed in the movements of the body.

18. Wikipedia. 2019. Fête Galante. https://en.wikipedia.org/wiki/Fête_galante (accessed 29.08.2019). Note: *Fête Galante* is a category of painting created by the French Academy in 1717 to describe Antoine Watteau's (1684–1721) variations on the theme of the *Fête Champêtre*, which featured figures in ball dress or masquerade costumes frolicking in parkland settings. After the death of Louis XIV in 1715, the aristocrats of the French court abandoned the grandeur of Versailles for the more intimate townhouses of Paris where, elegantly attired, they could play and flirt and put on scenes from the Italian commedia dell'arte. Fête Galante paintings are an important part of the Rococo period of art, which saw the focus of European arts move away from the hierarchical, standardized grandeur of the church and royal court and toward an appreciation for intimacy and personal pleasures. (…) By portraying his patrons in scenes reminiscent of the mythologized land of Arcadia, where humans had supposedly lived in leisurely harmony with nature, Watteau was able to get his paintings the highest ranking at the Académie and still flatter his buyers.
19. Roland Barthes, *Fragments d'un discours amoureux,* (Paris: Éditions du Seuil, 1977). Note: Ravishment: episode deemed initial during which the subject is in love "ravished" (captured and enchanted) by the image of the beloved object.
20. Wikipedia. 2019. "Inertia." https://en.wikipedia.org/wiki/Inertia. (accessed 29.08.2019). Note: Inertia is the resistance of any physical object to any change in its velocity. This includes changes to the object's speed or direction of motion. An aspect of this property is the tendency of objects to keep moving in a straight line at a constant speed when no forces act upon them. In common usage, the term "inertia" may refer to an object's "amount of resistance to change in velocity" (which is quantified by its mass), or sometimes to its momentum, depending on the context. The term "inertia" is more commonly understood as shorthand for "the principle of inertia", as described by Newton in his first law of motion: an object not subject to a net external force moves at a constant velocity. Thus, an object will continue moving at its current velocity until a force causes its speed or direction to change. On the surface of the Earth, inertia is often masked by gravity and the effects of friction and air resistance, both of which tend to decrease the speed of moving objects (commonly to the point of rest). This misled Aristotle to believe that objects would move only as long as force was applied to them.

21. Wikipedia. 2019. "The Salon." https://en.wikipedia.org/wiki/The_Salon. (accessed 29.08.2019). Note: The Salon is a gathering of people under the roof of an inspiring host, partly to amuse one another and partly to refine the taste and increase the knowledge of the participants through conversation. These gatherings often consciously followed Horace's definition of the aims of poetry, "either to please or to educate." One important place for the exchange of ideas was the salon. The word *salon* first appeared in France in 1664 (from the Italian word *salone*, itself from *sala*, the large reception hall of Italian mansions). Literary gatherings before this were often referred to by using the name of the room in which they occurred, like *cabinet, réduit, ruelle,* and *alcôve*. Before the end of the 17th century, these gatherings were frequently held in the bedroom (treated as a more private form of drawing room): a lady, reclining on her bed, would receive close friends who would sit on chairs or stools surrounding her.

Tar's Second Insertion

THE OSCILLATING MOTION

In 1940, metaphysician John Wheeler stated that what we consider to be matter can be a single electron that moves back and forth over time and thus embodies all matter.[1] Wheeler, who was part of a scientific development that investigated the essence of matter and time, must have empathized with the character of Tar when he came up with this hypothesis: Wheeler imagined a movement of matter that would allow the particle to become omnipresent. The movement and its object, the matter and its dynamics, are collaborating without inherent incentive. The single electron would be dragged along for the ride. The motion needs a speck of mass to complete its trajectory. According to Wheeler, they could make up the whole of reality. They would do it without time or consciousness.

      Sight from *The Golden Apartment,* high noon: today the sun is out. It has joined forces with the troposphere for some heavy lifting. The boats are playing with the caterpillars, but seem to be at a disadvantage underneath the clear sky. The field is being radiated with abundant UV and infrared. Tar particles rise in thick low fumes, too heavy to float. The smog lingers on the plot for a brief moment. The sun orchestrates. Particles that do not get enough energy to be swallowed up by the heavens will be swept up by the gathering occluded front. Speaking of which, it seems that the clouds have arrived. The mortal organics have a less dramatic approach than their celestial counterparts. They steadily remove pollutants, while bringing in low-grade petroleum derivatives for the new pathway. Tar cannot be used for any other purpose, as it is not pure enough. But here it will do. It is mixed with sand for its final use. After that, it will be kind of useless. You cannot recycle sandy Tar, for it is too polluted.

The Anxious Explorer suggested once or twice that it could perhaps still be fired up. Perhaps the right circumstances could be created in a small-scale experiment. But you would need a lot of additional heat to ignite the fire. She may have tried it with small pieces a few times. In real life, it would have to be the perfect storm. Even the material should somehow show some leniency.

More recently pieces of Tar have also shown up on social media accounts:

_Digging for Tar with @thelobbyist. Here are some nice pieces found near the pigeon coop at a depth of 273 cm and 322 cm. More soon !! #geology #lobbying #active currency

_Strong concentrations of Tar at a depth of 121 cm and 275 cm in the northwest corner of the plot. Great spectacle!! #caterpillars #BobSmithson #smellscape

1. Matt O'Dowd, "The One-Electron Universe | Space Time." YouTube video, 12:49. "PBS Space Time," 10.08.2017 https://www.youtube.com/watch?v=9dqtW9MslFk (accessed 7.09.2019).
Note: Konstantina, Theodoridou, Danae and Protopapa, Efrosini (eds.) "The Rock, the Butterfly, the Moon and the Cloud". Notes on Dramaturgy in an ecological Age", "The Practice of Dramaturgy: Working on Actions in Performance, (Amsterdam, Valiz, 2017), 235 – 245.

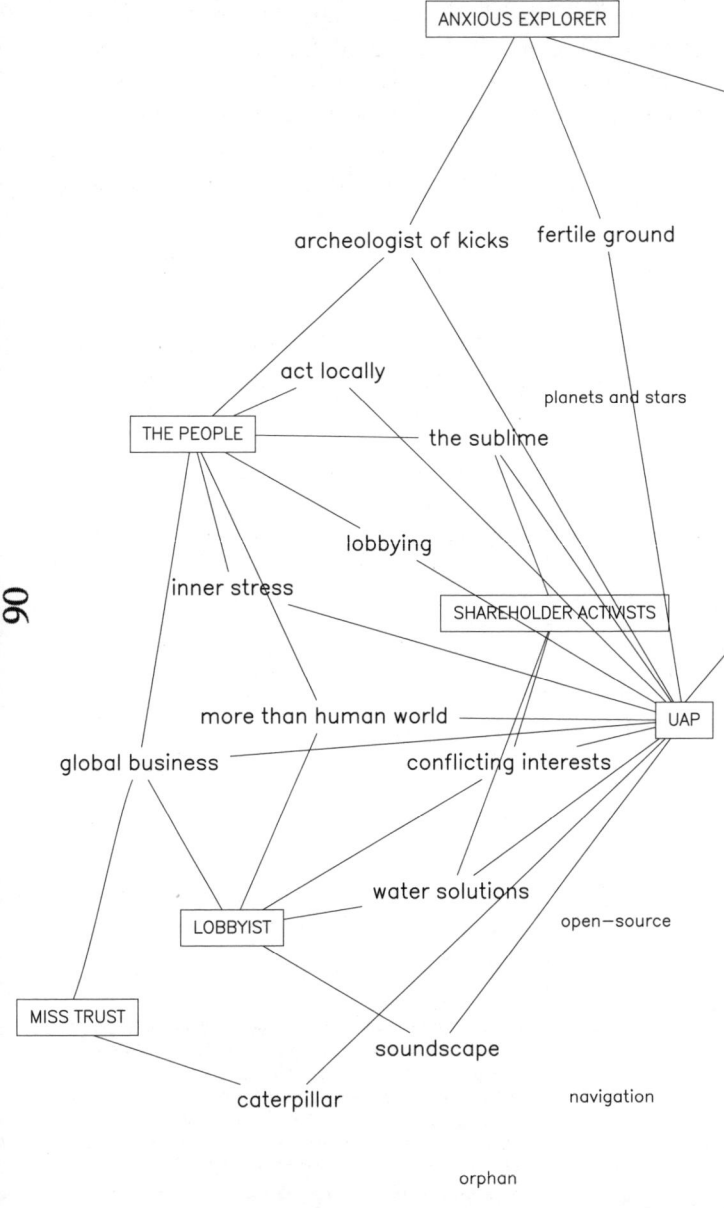

UAP (Undisciplined Advanced Practitioner)

hyper—mobile youthful prophets

resonance

ritual

revolutionary role

ethnobotany

Aquatic biology of the Self

healing topics   rescaling humanity

aseptic garden

flood   mortal organics

negotiation

carbon storage

dominant fictions

decision—making process

eco—system

entropy

The UAP is interested in navigation, urbanism, ethnobotany, and water solutions. Those in her social circle (both past and present) all have a tendency for gambling addictions—not in the sense of casino-like environments, or the non-places described by theorists like Marc Augé, but rather as in the sense of 'archaeologists of kicks'.[1] The UAP is educated in social sciences and super-modernity.

The entire Tondelier site is flooded. Only the two upper floors of the super luxury flats are habitable. The UAP developed sophisticated, high-tech water skills to move in a comfortable and dandyish elegant way through the environment. Her hobby is synchronized acrobatic free diving, and she is a member of *Aquatic Biology of the Self*—a local self-improvement group combining DIY diving techniques with leadership and diplomatic skills. In this group, the UAP meets the Shareholder Activists with a common interest in the sublime aesthetics of the propaganda art and black & white imagery of Leni Riefenstahl's Olympia. The UAP is involved in the lobby and counter-lobby of rewriting a covenant that includes all parties associated with the site.

Because of the floods Tondelier now hosts an extensive variety of native and exotic species. Some are quite invasive. The most remarkable species are a range of exotic vertebrates. These vertebrates, 'the invaders of the land', are a new kind of intermediates in search of the unheard, the now to come new resonance of the area. The UAP is interested in the abilities and sensitivities these vertebrates have developed in their new habitat of Tondelier. Rather than bridging with new citizens and adjacent areas, the vertebrates developed a slow tunnelling potential. The UAP has a reputation among her peers and different characters in Tondelier as a lunatic and a pathological idiot due to her attempts at defining the 'new resonance' for Tondelier. Only The Set, in the form of the flood (power and energy of water), and the vertebrates can support and understand this resonance, because this resonance was hitherto absent, invisible, and unheard. Maybe it was not part of the plan ... But not only resonance was missing; Tar was also absent. Only on warm days does its smell spread sluggishly into the social cohesion. Tar is absently silent, and this feels suspicious to the UAP.

When storms blow over the site, strong currents, micro tsunamis, and other (un)natural disturbances take control. Then the vertebrates become guides of sorts, who manage and predict water and wind, and apply the knowledge of the traditional Feng Shui methods as concrete solutions. The UAP developed these methods while traveling through old Persian libraries, where she was engaged in historical bookbinding and restoration, inspired by her fascination with Shen Kuo's Dream Pool Essays.[2]

It was the time she still lived with her father, the owner of a luxury pigeon hotel and resort in the Caribbean and Emirates. The UAP lost her mother at a very young age and was raised by several mistresses, governesses, secretaries, and assistants of her father's company. Raised by all forms of kin, with corporate love and care, while inbreeding heroic messenger pigeons, is for the UAP a convention.[3] She had an affair with Elisabeth, the mother of Miss Trust, which came to an abrupt end due to the tragic accident of Elisabeth and Carl Harold Trust.

The UAP navigates between all groups in the Tondelier site. She uses her skills and sensitivities for building a more than human world, as the different groups living in the upper levels of the buildings are falling apart. Connecting all involved parties, the UAP uses the ideas and protocols based on the *Alliance of Wild Ethics:* relations that unfold on the site as a space of quest instead of conquest.[4] She is the co-founder of a Tondelier covenant where future protocols are at stake using the 'garden' as a concept and 'principles of permaculture' as a methodology.

The UAP is surrounded by a cloud of ambiguity and opacity. She is involved in some serious healing and reconciliation on the site, but it is unclear if she was aware of or even involved in the corruption scandals and drama's that had occurred on the site in the last decade. For example, before the flood there was a fancy restaurant which served local toxic food and poisoned local citizens. Some illegal Bulgarian workers drowned. Some of these bodies are currently composting on site, and becoming part of the flourishing wildlife ecology and fungal reproduction.

The UAP has been increasingly active in lobbying for environmental justice. She is aware of the potential space for wildlife, as opposed to the imaginary doom scenario for humanity, created by the flood. While the surrounding waters reconnect the Scheldt river basin and the North Sea, dominant invasive exotic species are spreading over West European waters at an increasing rate. The city of Ghent, the Tondelier site, and the contiguous waterway De Lieve can play a revolutionary role in the future, when water will be part of an holistic governance 2.0, a model for living together with and within other entities.[5] The covenant drafted by the UAP contains some of these ideas: visionary concepts on the craft of negotiating and dealing with water. The UAP is inspired by, and admires, the tactics of historical figures such as Margaretha van Constantinople and Shen Kuo. Historical figures aware of the political, economic, and scientific powers humanity owes to the energy and values of water in all its possible forms.[6]

1. Marc Augé, *Non-Places. Introduction to an Anthropology of Super-modernity* (London, New York: Verso, 1995).
2. Wikipedia. 2019. "Dream Pool Essays." https://en.wikipedia.org/wiki/Dream_Pool_Essays (accessed 29.08.2019). Wikipedia. 2019. "Shen Kuo." https://en.wikipedia.org/wiki/Shen_Kuo (accessed 29.08.2019). Note: Dream Pool Essays is a Chinese classical and extensive

book written by the polymath and statesman of the Song dynasty Shen Kuo (1031 – 1095). Excelling in many fields of study and statecraft, he was a mathematician, astronomer, meteorologist, geologist, zoologist, botanist, pharmacologist, agronomist, archaeologist, ethnographer, cartographer, encyclopedist, general, diplomat, hydraulic engineer, inventor, academy chancellor, finance minister, governmental state inspector, poet, and musician. He was the head official for the Bureau of Astronomy in the Song court, as well as an Assistant Minister of Imperial Hospitality. He compiled Dream Pool Essays, an enormous work, while isolated on his lavish garden estate. Dream Pool Essays consists of some 507 separate essays exploring a wide range of subjects. At the time, China was a centre of monetary, military, and scientific advancement. During the Song Dynasty (960-1271), paper money, movable type printing, the hydraulic clock, firearms, and the magnetic compass were invented. This is described in his Dream Pool Essays. Shen was the first to describe the magnetic needle compass, which would be used for navigation. He created the concept of true north, understood in terms of magnetic declination towards the north pole, through experimentation of suspended magnetic needles and "the improved meridian determined by Shen's [astronomical] measurement of the distance between the pole star and true north." This was a decisive step in human history to make compasses more useful for navigation, although it likely remained unknown in Europe for another four hundred years. Following an old tradition in China, Shen created a raised-relief map while inspecting borderlands.

3. "Army of Love," https://thearmyoflove.net/about (accessed 29.08.2019).

4. "Alliance for Wild Ethics," https://wildethics.org/ (accessed 29.08.2019).

5. Wikipedia. 2019. "Lieve (kanaal)." https://nl.wikipedia.org/wiki/Lieve_(kanaal) (accessed 29.08.2019).

6. Wikipedia. 2019. "Margaret of Constantinople." https://nl.wikipedia.org/wiki/Margaretha_II_van_Vlaanderen (accessed 29.08.2019). Note: In 1251, the Countess of Flanders, Margaret of Constantinople, aka Margaret "The Black Lady" of Flanders, gave permission to dig the Canal De Lieve, a connecting waterway between Ghent via Damme / the Zwin and the North Sea. Due to progressive silting of the Zwin, which was originally the tidal channel on the Belgian coast of the North Sea, the Canal De Lieve became unusable. Due to the interfluvium of the drainage basin of the North Sea and the river Scheldt basin (the river basin to which Ghent/Leie also belongs) several control locks/tide locks where necessary to bridge. These locks are better known as 'Rabot'.

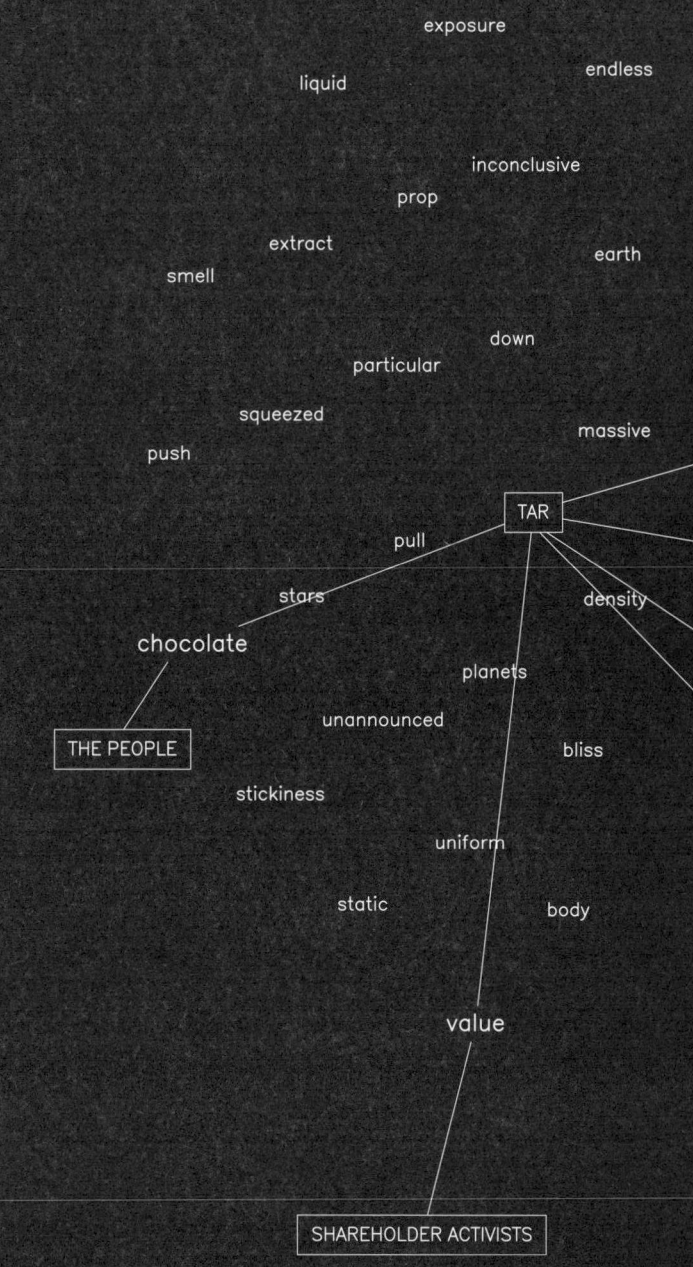

Tar's End

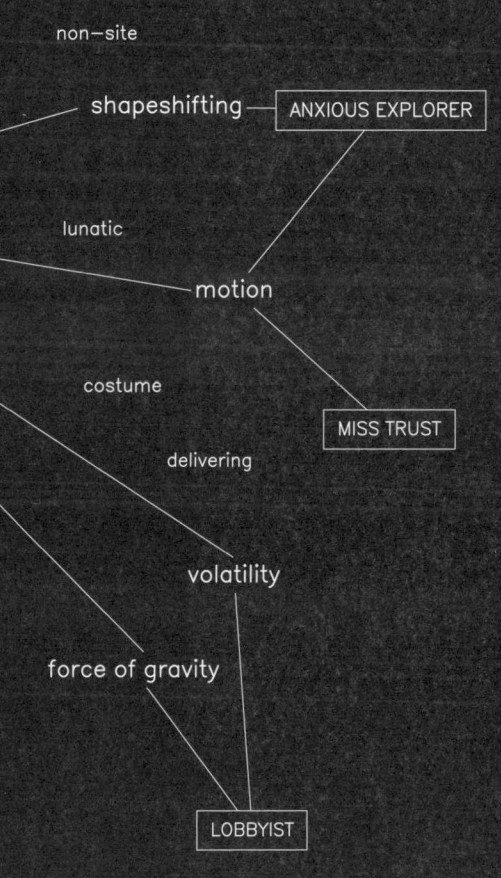

pace

non-site

shapeshifting — ANXIOUS EXPLORER

lunatic

motion

costume

MISS TRUST

delivering

volatility

force of gravity

LOBBYIST

NOT SO SUDDEN URGENCY

Petrified hydrocarbons such as Tar need time. No, they resist time. The action is not to disappear. The Earth's crust is slowly collapsing as the planet cools and densifies. One day, tectonic plates or nifty mortal organics pierce the pressurized pocket and make it ooze back onto the surface. Transformed, fossilized. Still dead, but not like before. Present and sticky. Very present. Those who want it don't really want it. But it's so valuable, so versatile. They start moving it.

It is fairly certain that the Shareholder Activists have recently placed tokens. But being involved in different games at the same time, they tend to spread their attention and activity, which makes recent developments a bit odd. A lot of attention is suddenly shifted to the plot. There were even a couple of attempts to define The Set. Some mortal organic substances tend to ruthlessly speculate; they seem ignorant of the fact that they came up with the narratives themselves. Movements in the plot tend to burst out of nowhere.

Golden Salon Conference Poster:
HOW DOES TIME CREATE SUBSTANCE?
#1 Keynote: Speculative Finance on the Substance of Tar
#2 Keynote: Dominant Fictions
12.30 to 13.30 Lunch in *The Golden Apartment*
#3 A Brief Dissertation on Homeopathy: the Memory of Material by the Feng Shui Expert

(The afternoon had to be shortened after a minor disruption occurred during the thesis of the Feng Shui expert. It had become quite unclear why she had been invited to speak on this subject in the first place. Some attendees had taken offense at the statement that a record was kept of the movements of Tar.)

A SOLE DESIRE

A parameter had been spread out. Soil samples had determined that no residual Tar deeper than four meters had been left behind. The newest path produces green energy while joggers run over it. Ironically, carbon storage had proven to be the final step to get rid of the Tar altogether. All Tar is removed from the plot by now, loaded onto boats by caterpillars.

The UAP had previously taken a sample of Tar from the site. She intended to have it tested in a laboratory. She wanted to know its chemical content. But once Shareholder Activists had ordered the complete removal of Tar, her idea had faded. She had hung on to it—an affectionate act, if you will.

It couldn't possibly have mattered to Tar how much of it was present on the plot when it was moved. All of it was gone now. All but one sample. And this speck was now kept in a state of care by the UAP, impotent and motionless. As dead matter, Tar had endured endings in many forms: transformation, removal, deterioration. Facing its last bit of matter, Tar now realized its desired outcome.

Epilogue

This is a work of fiction. Names, characters, businesses, places, events, locales, and incidents are either the products of the authors' imagination or used in a fictitious manner. Any resemblance to actual persons, living or dead, or actual events is purely coincidental.[1]

Even The Set, the background against which all the characters in this book play their part, is fictional. "I can be a landscape, prop, costume, sound, smell. I can be a painting. I can be digital", says The Set about itself.

Yet, this book would not exist without the real situation on which this wild fantasy is constructed: the city development of Tondelier in Ghent, where at the moment of writing, the last residues of Tar are excavated and transported, and the first residents have moved into their newly built apartments. This real place is the subject and focus of the artistic platform *PILOOT* (see p. 9).

This collective publication is an extravagant projection into one of many possible futures. A future in which Tondelier is flooded and inhabited by new species of vertebrae, where collective rituals take shape on a daily basis and Feng Shui methods are offered as concrete solutions, where relationships form and fade out in a *Golden Apartment* that was a real proposal by artist Lotte Geeven of the art platform at Tondelier, but was never realized for political reasons.[2] In the fictional narrative *The Orphans of Tar, The Golden Apartment* finally has the opportunity to become a reality.

On a plot in a state of becoming, do all characters have the agency to share responsibility for its final narrative? As this book is an exercise in collective writing, here this is certainly the case. Even if the individual contributors worked on their own characters, they made an effort to interconnect their characters into a shared narrative. While this project materialized independently of the platform *PILOOT,* it precisely fulfills the ambition of what *PILOOT* aims to be: a place for interdependent reflection on the situation of Tondelier, a place to 'exercise' (for a future that will be real) and show that developing shared narratives between widely diverging characters is possible.

Such exercises may seem futile and powerless in the context of capital and city development. But the Anxious Explorer in this book reminds us of the possibility of the Butterfly Effect: according to chaos theory, it is possible for a tornado to be caused by the flapping of the wings of a butterfly.

Danielle van Zuijlen

---

1. "General copyright disclaimer," the book designer, www.thebook designer.com/2010/01/6-copyright-page-disclaimers-and-giving-credit/ (accessed 05.09.2019).
2. "Meer dan object," Issuu, pp. 91-94, https://issuu.com/vlaams bouwmeester/docs/kio_web (accessed 08.09.2019). Note: Published on 11 December 2015 at the occasion of the symposium at KVS, Brussels, 'Verbeelding en publiek domein. Mogelijkheden van kunst in opdracht' (Imagination and the public space. Possibilities for art on commission).

APE#151

*The Orphans of Tar –
A Speculative Opera*
Julien de Smet, Ronny Heiremans, Heike Langsdorf, Vanessa Müller, Filip Van Dingenen, Stijn Van Dorpe, Clémentine Vaultier, Katleen Vermeir

© 2019 Art Paper Editions & editors (Alex Arteaga, Heike Langsdorf)
© 2019 of the texts and graphics: the contributors
All rights reserved, including the right of reproduction in whole or in part in any form.

ISBN 9789493146327
www.artpapereditions.org
First edition of 500 copies

*The Orphans of Tar –
A Speculative Opera*
is the third book of the series *Choreography as Conditioning*.

Series concept
Alex Arteaga
Heike Langsdorf

Contributors
Co-authoring collective of *The Orphans of Tar – A Speculative Opera:* Julien de Smet, Ronny Heiremans, Heike Langsdorf, Vanessa Müller, Filip Van Dingenen, Stijn Van Dorpe, Clémentine Vaultier, Katleen Vermeir. Danielle van Zuijlen (epilogue) and Gijs de Heij (graphics)

Copy Editor
Tawny Andersen

Graphic design
6'56"

Printed and bound in Tallinn.

Choreography as Conditioning is produced in the framework of the research project *Distraction as Discipline—an investigation into the function of attention and participation in performance art and art pedagogy* conducted by Heike Langsdorf in association with Anna Luyten at KASK / School of Arts, University College Ghent. The research project is financed by the Arts Research Fund of Diversity College Ghent.

All rights reserved. No part of this publication may be reproduced or transmitted in any form or by any means, electronic or mechanical, including photocopy, recording or any other information storage or retrieval system, without prior permission in writing from the publisher and the editors.